AF583614

The new Platform Papers

What future for the Arts in a post-Pandemic World?

Volume 1
December 2021

Julian Meyrick
General Editor

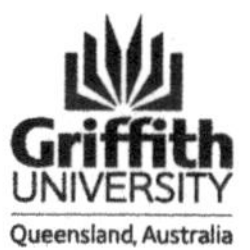

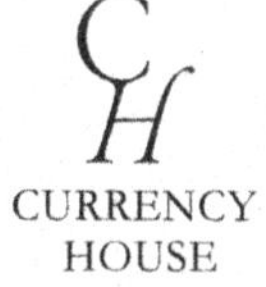

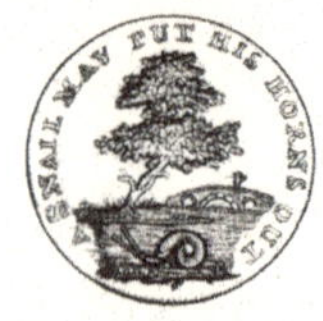

A snail may put his horns out

THOMAS SPENCE (1750–1814) was an English radical who campaigned against private ownership of land. He argued instead for a system of democratic parishes. He was also a passionate believer in equality between the sexes. He was particularly active in the 1790s when he produced a radical magazine, *Pig Meat, or Lessons for the Swinish Multitude* from his book shop in High Holborn, London. He also produced a series of tokens, many of which carry radical messages. Some of these were overt—one bore an image of William Pitt the Younger's head stuck on a maypole surrounded by dancing revellers. Others, however, were more subtle. He was fond of combining animals with political slogans. 'A Snail May Put His Horns Out' was a reminder that even the most powerless have the ability to affect change through resistance.

Hamish Maxwell-Stewart

Contents

Foreword:
What's New About the New Platform Papers?

Julian Meyrick
Yugarabul, Yuggera, Jagera and Turrbal country

Welcome to the New Platform Papers, an annual volume of essays written by and about the work of creative arts practitioners in Australia. As for so many people, our activities were severely disrupted by the Covid-19 pandemic in 2020–21. While our publication schedule was suspended, we restructured and reorganised. It is my great pleasure to introduce here, as General Editor, the current series, the successor to the original Platform Paper essays.

I joined the Editorial Committee of the Platform Papers in 2012, and have watched, over the years, as they have acquired the important public profile they have today. The final issue of the original series, no. 63, is written by our founder and patron,

Katharine Brisbane. *On the Lessons of History* looks back over the history of Currency House, the topics of the individual essays and the developments that have taken place in the arts in Australia over twenty years. It is reprinted in this volume. One of our authors, Mark Williams, has called the essay series 'Australia's Green Papers'. It is an apposite description. A Green Paper is a discussion paper presented by a minister before an important debate in Parliament. It is not a declaration of political views, but a basis for discussion that outlines options for consideration by Parliament and the general public. More than a summary or an opinion piece, and different from a manifesto or a consultancy report, each Platform Paper has one overriding task: to make its readers think more deeply about what it is saying. Platform Papers are about opening up public conversation, adding to our social stock of ideas, showing how values, arguments and action go together in addressing the burning questions in arts and culture, and through arts and culture, in the world beyond.

Over nearly twenty years, the series had developed a rhythm that I suspect reflects the heartbeat of the cultural sector itself. Out of the four Platform Papers we have published annually in the past, two would focus on art form-based concerns, and two on broader social and political issues. There was no hard and fast rule about the two categories, nor was it always the case that practising artists would write the first kind of essay, and academic researchers, the second. But they felt to me like the systole and diastole of Australian arts and culture, the cardiac cycle that keeps ideas new and old circulating around the system and people talking to each other. As a Platform Paper author twice myself, I copped my share of critical comment and pushback. But, in the words of a councillor of a remote community I heard speak in 2019, 'if people are complaining, you know they care'.

'New' is a stern, Modernist moniker that has become almost a traditional add-on in the arts. It juggles awareness of the value of history on the one hand, with hope for future transformation on the other. In the twentieth century we find 'the New Criticism', 'the New Architecture', 'the Nouveau Roman', and, in Australia, 'the New Wave'. The 'new' in the New Platform Papers reflects not so much a step-change in the essays *per se*, as an awareness that the context in which they will be written and read has fundamentally altered. It is the newness of the moment we are living in that imparts fresh energy and urgency to the series. But not yet, perhaps, a clear sense of direction.

What has it meant, this strange hiatus in our lives? What will we say about it once it has gone? This pandemic, which we have endured in isolation, has impacted upon us collectively. It is entirely reasonable to hesitate to say what might come next, especially for arts and culture. Will the 'pivot to online' continue or will there be a rush back to the sociability of live performance as soon as it is legally allowed? Will the debates about diversity that have erupted in the media, and sometimes in the street, effect systemic change? And for arts organisations, how can there be a return to 'business as usual' when so many of those 'businesses' are depleted of staff, talent, content and spirit? These questions are not going away. The 'new' in the New Platform Papers is an acknowledgment of this cold fact.

We also acknowledge the new reality artists now face in an important practical change. We have raised the fee for Platform Paper essays to the rate recommended by the Australian Society of Authors. This will amount to nearly $15,000 for a long essay.

The increase has been made possible by our restructure, and reflects our serious commitment to recognising the value of what creative practitioners have to say as writers as well as artists. A call for paper proposals will be announced on our new website.

The outlook of the new series remains essentially the same as the original, but the format is a little different. The first issue of the New Platform Papers published in this volume arose out of an event which will be central to the series from now on, an annual Authors' Convention. The Convention itself was the initiative of my colleague, the new Director of Currency House and Katharine's daughter, Harriet Parsons. A brilliant addition to our activities, the Convention is a two-day public gathering where we invite the authors of Platform Papers to come together to reflect on a given theme. A particular benefit is that there is scope to invite perspectives from younger practitioners. Our authors speak with the authority of practical experience and sustained reflection, but there are necessarily a limited number of them. The Convention is an opportunity to debate what lies ahead in a broad, inclusive and flexible way.

Harriet and I share an interest in the bigger policy picture in which arts and culture are immersed, and that is reflected in the theme of this year's Author's Convention: imagination, the arts and economics. We also believe that history matters—in particular, it matters to the future. Embracing the new, embracing change—real change, not just product change—is only possible when standing on the bedrock of a clear and acknowledged past. Our choice of authors has always given weight to those who have made a long-term contribution to the arts. Artists who write from experience about the work they do and how it contributes to Australia's social and political life often fall between two stools:

neither broad enough for the general reader nor academic enough for scholarly publication. There are other publications devoted to the arts, of good quality, on the visual arts, film and creative fiction, though they do not have the same remit as the Platform Papers. But in the nearly twenty years since we began publishing, many of these have fallen by the wayside.

For these reasons, the New Platform Papers will enlarge the scope of its essays. The original series focused on the performing arts. The new one will reflect the reality of greater crossover between art forms, expanding to encompass creative practice more generally. How we talk about our arts and culture is as important as the views we hold about them. This makes debate about their policy and practice doubly important. As we tack out of Covid-19 and into the Covid-affected years ahead, the New Platform Papers series is committed to giving space not just to the problems that have arisen, but to the new collective awareness we have acquired by solving them—or trying to: a collective awareness that will be expressed in our arts and culture if it can be expressed at all.

Season's Greetings

Katharine Brisbane
Cadigal country

Around 2001, when we established Currency House, I began writing a Christmas letter to my friends and family, reflecting on the year just past and what it meant, not just personally, but to us as a nation and even a global community. Currency House was to be my retirement project after I had stepped down as publisher of Currency Press. Over two decades I have continued to be grateful to you who have supported us, by writing for us, buying Platform Papers, coming to our events and donating to our cause. So I include all of you when I begin this year's letter, as I do every Christmas,

Dear Friends,

We have come to the end of a year that history is bound to see as the most unexpected, disruptive, and I hope, in the end most rewarding, intervention since Australia's colonial settlement. The pandemic has revealed how frail is the veil of the public good in the face of individual insistence. The capacity of self-interest to thwart good intentions has challenged our identity as a nation and exposed the fragility of our democracy. As a result, we now have the privilege of living in interesting times.

The revelations of 2021, the misbehaviour, and worse, in federal Parliament, and the public scandals that followed, have exposed the calibre of those we have chosen to represent us, and the shaky ground on which our democracy stands. But the exposure of our shortcomings has also become a mandate for new ideas and fresh initiative and we have before us now a unique opportunity, a brief chance, for debate, and a new direction in Australian governance. We are by no means alone in this. The power of the idea is infectious. Can we begin again?

The traumatic events of this year have highlighted signs of willingness to change. The catastrophic bushfires that started in Australia in 2019 were followed by the like in 2020–21 in California and Canada, Greece and Europe, confirming that our love affair with coal is finally over. In May, resistance to institutional racism gained new momentum when black American, George Floyd, died on a street in Minneapolis while a white police officer, Derek Chauvin, knelt on his neck. His slow suffocation over nine long minutes was captured on video and led to Chauvin's conviction for murder. In late 2020 Donald Trump was defeated by Joe Biden in the US election.

And to general relief the mild-mannered Democrat revealed a welcome capacity for vision and common sense. Despite sustained opposition from Trump's supporters, including an armed assault on Washington's Capitol on 6 January 2021, Biden has set about securing the future of his country with an economic agenda to rival FDR's New Deal.

On 26 January, Grace Tame set a new path for young women when she accepted the award for Australian of the Year. In February, her campaign on behalf of survivors of sexual assault inspired Brittany Higgins to report her rape by a fellow staffer inside Parliament House. Brittany's courageous and steadfast account set off a wave of historical reporting from other women and their friends. In March Cabinet Minister Christian Porter identified himself as the subject of an allegation of rape dating back to his university days; and then in April Christine Holgate appeared in suffragette white before a parliamentary enquiry into her removal from Australia Post.

In May, allegations of money laundering through Crown Casinos led to James Packer being found unfit to hold a casino licence in NSW, and prompted a second investigation in Victoria. The Brereton Report into alleged war crimes by Australian troops in Afghanistan also came back into the news when Ben Roberts-Smith, a veteran of the SAS decorated with the Victoria Cross, sued three Australian Newspapers for defamation. Judgment is yet to be passed on his case, but the exposure of activities that have been shrouded in secrecy, whether in the police, gambling or the military, feels like change towards a healthier country.

In September, the unilateral decision of the US to withdraw its troops from Afghanistan, ended the 20-year conflict in chaos. Kabul immediately fell to the Taliban and those who fled were abandoned at the airport. Sixty were killed in a terrorist attack.

These revelations of 2021 have raised growing doubts in Australia about how we are perceived as a middle-sized world power internationally. At the time of writing, France has withdrawn its ambassador from Australia after a contract for a fleet of submarines, worth $90 billion, was summarily cancelled by Canberra. The project had been expected to take fifteen to twenty years. It has been replaced by a new contract with the US and UK, this time for nuclear submarines, covering a further two decades. The staggering cost of submarines always comes as a surprise, but what is more remarkable is the willingness of our government to engage in long-term planning when it comes to military expansion. The constraints of the three-year election cycle vanish when it comes to submarines. What if we also made 20-year investment plans—for climate change mitigation, or education, health, welfare, culture, employment? And what about Aboriginal reconciliation? These things urgently need to be debated.

Domestically, we shall all be grateful to see the end of 2021. As we had been to see the end of 2020. This time last year, the borders were threatening to close, so our family gathered early for Christmas—on 6 December. We had three generations around the table, glad to be together in the flesh. Afterwards, I watched as Sydney's streets grew heavy with anxiety, frustration and traffic; then, on Christmas day itself, eerily desolate. This year the odds for a family Christmas are better; although the situation in Melbourne is worsening. In Sydney we are still in lockdown, so I haven't seen my children, Nick and Harriet, for months. But we talk on the phone and on Zoom, and I'm comfortably settled in my own home, so I have the best of things as they are. My granddaughters Adelash and Aynalem are near at hand and keep an eye on me. They have both turned 30 now, and are making their way in life. And this year we look forward to having four generations at Christmas: in November Aya and her partner Dion plan to make me a great-grandmother. Now that is both a gift and an achievement.

Greetings to you all for a peaceful Christmas,

Katharine

Imagination, the Arts and Economics

NO. 1

December 2021

Edited by
Julian Meyrick
and Harriet Parsons

Thanks

To our partners who answered the call to support our authors with their donations:

Katharine Brisbane, AM
Elizabeth Butcher, AM
Sally Crawford
Penny Chapman
Wayne Harrison, AM
Geoffrey Rush, AC
Caroline Verge
Rachel Ward, AM and Bryan Brown, AM
Kim Williams, AM

The authors who kindly donated their writing:

Jonathan Biggins
Katharine Brisbane
Ian Maxwell
Hamish Maxwell-Stewart
Julian Meyrick
Harriet Parsons

The School of Literature, Art and Media and the CREATE Centre of the University of Sydney for hosting the inaugural convention of Platform Papers authors.

Introduction: A Snail May Put His Horns Out

Harriet Parsons
Wurundjeri country

For artists, the rungs on the career ladder between poverty and wealth are few and far between. Success and celebrity go together. It is difficult to think of another profession in which the middle is so insecure. But artists, especially performers, are masters at disguising their injuries: physical, emotional, psychological and economic. In public, they dance before our eyes, like butterflies on fragile wings, but behind the glamour they bear the scars of a life exposed to risk. Since the 1980s Australia has become one of the wealthiest countries in the world, but, for the arts, the national prosperity has felt more like austerity. At times it has felt like outright hostility. The present moment is a case in point: in 2020, at the very time arts workers were left out of the

JobKeeper program, the Minister for Education doubled the cost of a degree in the humanities while reducing the cost of degrees in the so-called STEM subjects.

Harnessing the power of celebrity to protest against these assaults means risking personal abuse from an ugly social media or missing out on work in an unregulated industry; but the sector is also mute for a third reason: because somewhere along the line we lost the language to express what it is that we actually do for society, beyond selling entertainment and home decor. When the dust settles between the health professionals and the economists over 'the path out of Covid', it must become apparent that what we are really facing in this moment is not a crisis of health or financial management, but culture. We have to decide what changes we are willing to make if we are to plan a route, not just out of the pandemic, but off the dangerous course we have been following for the past forty years. The arts may seem an unlikely point man for this operation. We have become more like a snail than a butterfly, withdrawn inside the protection of its shell, but as the eighteenth-century radical Thomas Spence once wrote, 'a snail may put his horns out'.

This first volume of the New Platform Papers is devoted to exploring how our imaginations became captives of the 'dismal science', and the role the arts can play in leading the way out. Some time in the late 1970s or the early 1980s, Australians—colonial Australians—lost the confidence to debate our culture. For two centuries, we had explored our ambivalent relationship with this continent in art and literature. From Frederick McCubbin's haunting painting *Lost*, to the legend of the Kelly Gang; from CJ Dennis's larrikin sentimental bloke, to the hallucinatory disorientation of Kenneth Cook's

Wake in Fright; from AA Phillip's unflinchingly self-critical coining of 'the cultural cringe' to Donald Horne's sarcastic 'the lucky country', we tried to find our sense of direction in its alien landscape. Yet our ambivalence was also a source of strength. Our willingness to interrogate the legitimacy of our Australian national identity created a foundation on which we felt entitled to question the authority of others, and fostered a spirit of egalitarianism that, by the 1980s, was widely accepted as definitively Australian.

Though the larrikin spirit of equality was selective, the principle was sound, but in the 1980s it became a new animal. Laconic self-deprecation was replaced by a more self-congratulatory individualism. The old ambivalence was branded 'unAustralian'—an echo of 'unAmerican' which our neighbours across the Tasman were spared ('un-New Zealandy' just didn't have the same ring). The new brand of flag-waving nationalism that Bob Hawke championed as prime minister was spurred on by the impending anniversary of two-hundred years of colonisation. Billed as the 'celebration of a nation', the festivities of 1988 included a flotilla of tall ships re-enacting the arrival of Arthur Phillip's first fleet in Sydney Harbour, 'Coca Cola' emblazoned across the sails of their flagship. The impression the performance made on Parliament is recorded in Hansard:

MR FAIRBANKS:	As far as I am aware, I think everybody on the staff of the Authority thought that the Tall Ships were wonderful.
SENATOR BISHOP:	You also hear statements that without the First Fleet, Australia Day on 26 January

	would not have had the emotional charge that it did.
MR FAIRBANKS:	I have heard that statement made.
SENATOR BISHOP:	Have you also heard a statement made that it was a shame that there had to be a Coca Cola sign on one of the ships?
MR FAIRBANKS:	I have heard that too.[1]

Over the decade-and-a-half from 1983 to 1996, the visionary leadership of Bob Hawke and his treasurer and successor, Paul Keating, transformed the nation. On coming to power, Hawke backed the conservationists and blocked the Franklin Dam in Tasmania. Ten years later, when Keating became prime minister, he delivered his famous Redfern speech, publicly acknowledging to Australia's Aboriginal people, 'We committed the murders. We took the children from their mothers.'[2] But another side of their vision was a wave of structural reforms that shifted national government away from the Westminster system, with its Whitehall arms-length style of bureaucracy, towards a semi-American 'Senior Executive Service'. Market economics went from an explanatory theory, to an ideology that pervaded every aspect of government decision-making.

The sociologist Michael Pusey documented its progress through the bureaucracy in Canberra from 1985 to 1986. In the published results he concluded in 1991:

> At the boundary of what was once a friendly and intelligent Australian federal bureaucracy ... there is instead an insulating distance that protects the political-administrative system from both intellectual and 'ordinary' culture, and so from participation, from

> interpretations of need, and from many of the normal and supposedly normative prerogatives and entitlements of citizenship in a liberal social democracy.[3]

Economic rationalism was imperturbable in its self-confidence: the market economy was an all-encompassing, autonomous system, with government—and the corporate world it sought to emulate—observers from outside. Pusey's quarrel was not with economics *per se* but rather the underlying 'scientism' of economic rationalism 'that seems to turn arbitrariness into givenness and imperiously asserts its own exclusive evaluative criteria for what will, in the wake of its "reforms", count as intelligence, ability, and efficacy within and beyond Canberra'.[4]

The positivism of economic rationalism allowed its followers to level the charge of 'relativism' against judgments reached through deliberative processes. Critical evaluation was displaced by quantitative measures such as ticket sales and auction prices, especially in relation to public funding. Some in the arts and humanities reacted against the commodification of the 'intrinsic' values of culture by asserting the authority of their own subjectivity. In an unlikely twist, French post-structuralist philosophers became celebrities with cult status. In 1992 Jacques Derrida lectured to sell-out shows in Sydney and Melbourne.

The two-pronged attack on the arts—both administrative and conceptual—had a paralysing effect on cultural debate generally. Elevating economics to the plane of absolute knowledge and reducing critical judgment to an expression of personal interest polarised politics in Canberra too. As the 1990s became the 2000s it fomented a series of leadership coups, minority governments and ugly personal attacks in Parliament. The trend was brought up short in 2012 by Julia Gillard's impromptu 'misogyny speech', addressed to the leader of the opposition, Tony Abbott.

The application of market economics to sectors that are *not* market driven burnt out professionals committed to the public good, and enriched the powerful at the expense of the poor and vulnerable. Its effects in the major sectors of education, health, welfare and the arts were manifestly destructive, but it took the emergencies of the bushfires of 2019 and the pandemic the year following to bring home the folly of this 'market first' thinking. For forty years governments had succeeded in persuading us that the infrastructure of civil society was the icing on the cake of the business economy, but when the global economy came to a screeching halt in 2020, it was the non-market-driven sectors that pulled together and, with injections of public spending, kept our lives motoring along until business could recover.

Twice we have seen this in recent years: in 2008, in the wake of the Global Financial Crisis, and again in 2020–21. On both occasions, Australian governments have accrued a national debt of 'unprecedented size' and neither time has the sky fallen in. The positive effects of government debt on business—through the JobKeeper scheme—came as an especially great surprise. The dawning realisation that something was seriously wrong with government's approach to economics resulted in a wave of new books, articles and interviews with economists, explaining the benefits of national 'debt', and proposing schemes that only a year before would have been inconceivable: a universal basic income, a negative income tax, a universal jobs guarantee.

It is for all these reasons that this first volume of the New Platform Papers is devoted to the role of the imagination in economics, and what economists need to learn from artists in order to use that faculty better. The essays in the first issue were delivered at the inaugural Currency House Authors' Convention in July 2021. The theme for the Convention was inspired by Richard Bronk's book *The Romantic Economist* (2009). Richard began his career in the financial sector, including a stint as an Adviser to the Bank of England, before becoming a philosopher in the history of economic thought. Consequently he takes an approach to economics that is familiar in the creative arts: exploring the field through its *practices*. The key metaphor of *The Romantic Economist* was conceived by the poet Samuel Taylor Coleridge: that the mind is a lamp that in part creates what it sees by the light it sheds. The new worlds that economists envisage are neither entirely imaginary, nor entirely objective. They are a combination of both: a partial view of the world that is revealed by the 'lamp' of their ideas.

As our second speaker, the renowned economist John Quiggin explained, the *history* of economic thought—how economic ideas and theories have changed from Adam Smith to the present day—does not form part of a standard economics degree today. With no view of the eccentric trail of trial and error behind them, it is hardly surprising that contemporary economists should imagine their discipline is infallible. Economists study the forces that drive social behaviour as a whole, rather than individual intentions. Early proponents of modern market economics counteracted the hubris that such a 'god's-eye-view' of humanity might instil with strong doses of satire. So we invited the satirist Jonathan Biggins to join John Quiggin in a conversation about two works that were predecessors to Smith's *Wealth of Nations*, Bernard Mandeville's *The Fable of the Bees* and Jonathan Swift's

A Modest Proposal. Both imagine a fanciful world in which economic principles supplant moral values. In Mandeville's hive, busy bees abandon virtue to pursue their own self-interests. The consumer society they create is a world of untold luxury in which every commodity is shoddy and every institution corrupt. Swift's essay proposed to solve the problem of poverty in Ireland in 1729 by eating the children of the poor. I asked our speakers if it were possible that, given we live in a world in which banks have sold life insurance to the dead, that Mandeville and Swift's satirical predictions were coming true.

Our final speaker on day one of the Convention was Astrid Jorgensen, Director of Pub Choir—relaunched during the pandemic as Couch Choir. Astrid formed Pub Choir with her accompanist Waveney Yasso in 2017. The idea of organising pub-goers into *ad hoc* choirs was an unexpected commercial success, and became the foundational expression of her personal philosophy: that embracing the ordinary in art could produce extraordinary results. As she writes in her essay, no-one 'wins' in music. When musicians play or sing together, they 'compete' by listening to each other more closely. They enter into each other's performances and complement them with their own, creating improvisations in which the whole is greater than the sum of its parts. When Pub Choir became Couch Choir the singers began recording their parts at home. She then edited them together into a combined choral recording. As Astrid explains, despite their physical isolation, the social connection of music carried over into lockdown. Some sent her messages that Couch Choir had saved their lives.

Day two of the convention was given over to our authors. Ahead of time, we had asked them to reflect on what changes had taken place in their parts of the arts sector since their Platform Papers were published, and what new possibilities they saw ahead in a post-pandemic world. Their expertise ranges across disciplines and art forms, including theatre, music, film, the digital arts, cultural policy, law, economics and 'our ABC'. Their decades of knowledge and experience put the present challenges in the context of Australia's complex history, with a view to the cultural sector as a whole.

With some Platform Papers published as long ago as 2004, there were few younger practitioners in the grid of faces on Zoom. However, we saw this meeting of 'the old guard' as an important and necessary step to reopening Currency House: we wanted to consult our elders before we plunged ahead towards an uncertain future. The performing arts in particular are ephemeral, and too prone to forget each passing generation as it is overtaken by the next. By maintaining our living connection to the past through the annual Authors' Convention, we may be able to save the next generation of authors from reinventing the wheel, and help them instead to build upon it.

My introduction to this first issue has dwelt on the culture of 'colonial' Australians, because so much of what our nation has experienced over the past forty years seems to relate explicitly to the colonial need to escape its history. Paul Keating attributed the atrocities of the past to a failure of imagination—the imagination shapes our reality in the most concrete of ways. Since 1988, market economics have illuminated the way ahead with an even narrower shaft of light than the colonial lamp of our forebears. But it is important to remember that it is the distorting shadows cast by its single beam that are the cause of fear and confusion, not the light. By bringing more lamps to bear—from First Nations, from the arts and humanities and other disciplines, from across the generations, across cultures and life experiences—we can dispel the shadows and illuminate the path ahead.

Endnotes

1 Estimates Committee A. 31/10/1988, Department of the Prime Minister and Cabinet, Program 5–Australian Bicentenary, Subprogram 5.1-Australian Bicentennial Authority, Hansard.

2 Redfern Speech (Year for the World's Indigenous People), delivered in Redfern Park by Prime Minister Paul Keating, 10 December 1992. Australian Government, Department of Prime Minister and Cabinet, 'Transcripts from the Prime Ministers of Australia', Transcript ID 9514.

3 Michael Pusey, *Economic Rationalism in Canberra: a Nation Building State Changes its Mind* (Cambridge University Press, 1991, transferred to digital printing, 2003, DOI http://dx.doi.org/10.1017/CBO9780511597121), pp. 12–13

4 Ibid, pp. 10–11.

Models, Uncertainty and Imagination in Economics

Richard Bronk
United Kingdom

One of the few prejudices that many economists and artists share is to assume that economics and markets are the province of cold reason, dry empiricism, and the remorseless logic of mechanical calculation, optimal performance, and a tendency to equilibrium. If emotions play a part in markets, they are presumed to be the base emotions of personal greed—leading to exploitative behaviour—or irrational fear and exuberance, leading to unfortunate distortions in otherwise rational expectations. It is generally assumed that economics is—or at least should be—the province of scientific rationalism, with little intellectual or practical overlap with an artistic emphasis on the structuring and creative role of the imagination, let alone human empathy.

In this address, I argue that these widespread assumptions could not be more wrong.[1] Both sides of CP Snow's two culture's divide have underestimated the role that metaphors and models play in structuring economics and economic behaviour.[2] Both sides, too, have largely ignored the extent to which imagination drives the essential creativity of capitalist markets and makes the future radically uncertain; and they have overlooked the part played by the imagination in shaping the stories that motivate consumers and investors, engage their emotions, and help them navigate the uncertain future.

Indeed, the business of being an entrepreneur, or—within government—of developing good economic policy, is an *art*. It involves creativity and an imaginative openness to new ways of thinking, as well as large amounts of disciplined analysis. Economics and economic behaviour are the province of what William Hazlitt called 'a reasoning imagination', which applies the lessons of experience to possible futures created in the mind and enables us to make *judgments* about how to act when the future is uncertain.[3] At the same time, economics needs to involve the ability to empathise with—the better to judge—the imaginaries and narratives motivating those with whom we interact socially, economically or politically. If behaviour is structured by narratives—as I argue—then we can only predict or influence outcomes by 'reading' the stories that matter to others and trying to convince them of our own narratives of how the future *should* be.

I wrote a book a few years ago called *The Romantic Economist—Imagination in Economics*.[4] And, as one reviewer noted, 'It is hard to imagine a more oxymoronic title' for my apparently paradoxical effort to highlight the imaginative aspects of the dismal science.[5] But this effort sprang from my seventeen years of practical experience in markets and economic policy, which—perhaps because of an earlier university training in literature and philosophy—led me to become increasingly intrigued by the frequent mismatch between the way economists model economies and the way that markets and investors work in practice. It was a mismatch that prompted me to wonder if the theories of the nineteenth-century Romantic poets and philosophers about the role played by imagination and sentiment in perception, thought, and behaviour might have much to teach those studying markets.

Most economists rely on relatively static equilibrium models to make predictions—models that assume that economic agents optimise within given constraints, on the basis of rational expectations of a future that is predictable (at least in probability terms). But the entrepreneurs and investors I met as an investment manager were constantly engaged in thinking up novel strategies and products and seemed permanently challenged by uncertainty about the creative strategies of others. Confidence, a will-to-win, and an intuitive grasp of emerging patterns were clearly essential to these entrepreneurs facing the radical indeterminacy of a future that they and others were seeking to reshape. As the economist Joseph Schumpeter famously noted, the type of competition that counts most in markets comes from the 'new commodity, the new technology ... the new type of organisation'; and the consequent 'process of industrial mutation ... incessantly revolutionises the economic structure *from within*'. It is this process of 'Creative Destruction' that Schumpeter argued is 'the essential fact about capitalism'.[6] Think, for example, of the impact of the internet, mobile phones, and artificial intelligence over recent years. As the sociologist Jens Beckert puts it, the modern capitalist system is subject to constant change, novelty, and 'unending disruption of the present'.[7]

How then are economic agents meant to know what the future holds and optimise among well-defined options? The answer, of course, is that they cannot. When novelty and innovation abound both in the economy itself and in the economic policies guiding it, it is far from rational to assume, as economists generally do, that the future is a statistical shadow of the past; and it is quite fanciful to assume that—with enough data, the correct model, and sufficient market incentives—economic agents will be able to work out the *best* course of action, let alone to assume that—thanks to free-market exchange—their actions will collectively lead to the most mutually advantageous outcome possible. Instead, as Jens Beckert and I have pointed out, economic actors have no choice but to *imagine* the future *yet to be created* by how they and others envisage or will it to be. It is these imaginaries or 'fictional expectations' that enable us to act *despite* the uncertainty we all face; and—when crystalised into shared narratives and models—it is these imaginaries that help coordinate our actions with others. And, since narratives and models influence behaviour and help construct the future, they inevitably become instruments of government policy and market power. In this way, imagination turns out to be not only the root cause of much of the economic uncertainty we face but also one of our principal tools for coping with that uncertainty, projecting market power and influencing outcomes.[8]

Here is the first thing we can learn from the Romantic poets and philosophers: while they did not themselves, it is true, tend to focus on this aspect of markets any more than economists have, their general emphasis on the creative power of the imagination to visualise counterfactuals, come up with entirely novel ideas, and elaborate a new vision—or as the poet William Wordsworth put it, to 'build up greatest things / From least suggestions'—lies behind their insistence that rational calculation alone cannot explain human behaviour.[9] Moreover, as John Stuart Mill, the English philosopher and economist most influenced by the Romantics, reminded us: 'the imaginative emotion which an idea when vividly conceived excites in us, is not an illusion but a fact, as real as any of the other qualities of objects.'[10] Imaginaries and the emotions attached to them—for example, imagined holidays and anticipated pleasure—matter every bit as much to market prices and behaviour as they do in the rest of life.

Before I return to this role of narratives and economic models in 'performing' the future by motivating beliefs and behaviour, I want to draw attention to perhaps the greatest legacy of Romantic thought—a legacy that can help explain how economists and policymakers have become locked into a way of thinking about market's that is largely blind to the creativity and instability of economic activity and the power of imaginaries. The Romantics—influenced directly or indirectly by Immanuel Kant's account of the human mind necessarily reading into the *world-as-it-appears-to-us* certain structuring principles—understood that we never have unmediated access to brute reality. Rather our observation and analysis are structured by the particular languages, conceptual categorisations and metaphors used. Wordsworth linked the poet's imaginative ability to present things in a new and different light to the use of metaphor. But the genius of Wordsworth and his contemporary, Samuel Taylor Coleridge, was to see that the same process that is obvious when poets are consciously colouring their vision by the use of surprising metaphors is at work in everyday perception and analysis. For Coleridge, the imagination is the 'prime Agent of all human Perception';[11] and Wordsworth argued that the human mind 'half-creates' the world it sees and is a 'creator and receiver both'.[12] In other words, what we see is a co-creation of the sense data we receive and the interpretative frameworks our minds supply. It cannot be otherwise because we cannot make sense of brute reality, or see it as a collection of meaningful objects, unless our minds project a framework of interpretation provided by language, metaphor or model. As Coleridge put it, 'You must have a lantern in your hand to give light, otherwise all the materials in the world are useless, for you cannot find them, and if you could, you could not arrange them'.[13]

The relevance of this general truth for understanding the discipline of economics and its impact are manifold. For one thing, economics is, as Kurt Heinzelman noted, a 'resonant system of metaphor'.[14] Indeed, as Deirdre McCloskey pointed out in her book, *The Rhetoric of Economics*, economic theories are particularly saturated in metaphors—from demand 'curves' to 'game theory'.[15] Crucially, since many of these metaphors are no longer consciously recognised, they unconsciously structure the way economists think about markets. Take, for example, the notion of a market 'equilibrium'—a concept borrowed, as the historian of economics Philip Mirowski points out, from the less than obviously relevant field of nineteenth-century energy physics and applied metaphorically to dynamic capitalist markets.[16] Such metaphors, and the models based on them, help economists focus on some aspects of reality—in this case, the potential allocative efficiency of market exchange—but usually at the cost of limiting their ability to make sense of, or even notice, other aspects.

Equally crucially, it is not possible simply to rely on testing theoretical models (based on metaphor) against real-world facts as a fool-proof way of ensuring that economics is on the right track, because the data economists use is partly constructed by the particular data collection methods and conceptual frameworks applied. As the literary critic MH Abrams puts it in his book, *The Mirror and the Lamp*, facts (as the derivation of the word from the Latin *facta* implies) are 'things made as much as things found, and made in part by the analogies through which we look at the world as through a lens'.[17] In other words, the facts at our disposal cannot be an entirely objective touchstone for assessing the truth-value of an economic theory. While they matter enormously, of course, to the urgent business of assessing the relative merits of different theoretical constructions of reality, facts themselves are part-creations of theory and metaphor. This means that facts—almost as much as theoretical models—should always be seen as provisional artefacts.

The practical and policy implications of such Romantic epistemology are enormous. For if any theoretical framework or conceptual grid—such as that provided by standard equilibrium-based economics—has limitations as a way of parsing reality and making sense of it, it follows that reliance on any *one* such framework implies an inevitable bias or limitation in the way we see and analyse our predicament. The political scientist Wade Jacoby and I have summed up the dangers of such modelling monocultures like this:

> We need theories and conceptual structures to make sense of the chaos around us, in the same way that we need a lantern to see in the dark. Yet when we only have access to one theoretical or conceptual

> structure—one source of light—then our field of vision is likely to be severely limited and our analysis biased. It is for this reason that a monoculture—which involves the widespread internalization of one mental framework or model—is so dangerous. Even when a shared mental model is apparently the best available, reliance on this single model or framework implies that we will keep stumbling on aspects of reality we earlier missed, simply because these aspects lie outside the area illuminated by the framework or model we used.[18]

The perils of becoming locked into one way of analysing economic reality became painfully apparent during the financial crisis of 2008, when the global financial sector and national regulators had for the most part internalised a homogenous set of Value at Risk (VaR) models that—by confusing radical uncertainty with measurable risk—left the key players blind to early warning signs of a catastrophe that became, in retrospect, obvious. Likewise, central banks almost all used a type of dynamic stochastic general equilibrium (DSGE) model that simply assumed rational expectations, a tendency for markets to return to equilibrium and, most remarkably of all, actually ignored the financial sector and the possibility of default. It is not surprising that central bankers relying on such models mostly failed to spot emerging problems until too late. Likewise, many would argue that accounting practices and economic models that ignore environmental externalities have predisposed companies and governments to ignore the long-term costs of carbon emissions and other forms of pollution.

For this reason, perhaps the most urgent use of imagination in economics is to experiment with new metaphors and diverse modelling assumptions that can cast new light on complex multifaceted reality. For example, when economists apply epidemiological models metaphorically to the study of market contagion and financial panic, it helps them unearth key tipping points in highly interconnected financial networks; and it helps policymakers isolate highly connected institutions that may act as 'super-spreaders' of default risk. More generally, I would argue, businesses and government departments should be structured to encourage the disruptive insights provided by alternative models and theories; for, as Paul Feyerabend puts it, there 'exist facts which cannot be unearthed except with the help of alternatives to the theory' being tested.[19] If we want to detect unconscious interpretive biases in perception and analysis, we have to learn to hover between different conceptual frameworks. Indeed, if we want to avoid the perils of groupthink, we have to exhibit a version of what the poet, John Keats, called '*negative capability*'—the capacity to be in 'uncertainties, mysteries, doubts, without any irritable reaching after fact and reason'.[20]

Such receptiveness to new perspectives is also required when coping with uncertainty about the future—with the radical indeterminacy in economic systems caused by the constant interplay of the innovative strategies of myriad different actors. You can only spot emerging patterns in dynamically evolving complex market systems if you are receptive to new pointers and flexible in how you see the world. Such *passive* receptiveness to novelty is—I would argue—a necessary component of imaginative thinking about the economy; but on its own it is not, of course, sufficient. Entrepreneurs, investors, and policymakers also need to *actively* experiment with different models and metaphors and use them as *diagnostic tools* for unearthing new trends. At the same time, they need to *actively* work up any new solutions they imagine and subject them to a rigorous scientific and ethical audit.

This sort of eclectic use of diverse models and metaphors may be the basis of creative thinking in economics, but it has, of course, its practical limits. In the end, governments have to choose a policy, and companies must pursue a particular course. And, while they must remain aware of the limitations of their chosen approach and open to challenge internally, they often have little choice but to promote a consistent narrative and modelling framework to others if they wish to coordinate investment in their chosen goal and stabilise the expectations of those with whom they cooperate. The *art* of entrepreneurship and good government then is to balance the need for agreed modelling frameworks and shared narratives (that facilitate coordination by providing a shared logic of action and a common set of beliefs) with the need to avoid dangerously myopic groupthink and encourage the trial-and-error search for new solutions.

This balancing act is easier said than done because of the trade-off between the ability to influence outcomes by promoting a consistent message and the flexibility of outlook required to spot new trends and change course in light of them. The coordination properties of models and their associated narratives—their tendency when internalised to frame expectations and influence behaviour and outcomes—makes them an instrument of corporate or government power. And this power may—initially at least—be in inverse proportion to the degree of humility with which the narrative or model is promulgated. Central banks have wrestled with this problem when giving markets forward guidance. Their aim is usually to settle market expectations around a policy target and a route map towards it that their models suggest is feasible. But, if they are to maintain long-term credibility, central bankers must also leave themselves with enough internal and external discretion to adapt to new pointers and adjust their message accordingly.

There is another aspect of the Romantic conception of the imagination that is central to economic behaviour and the skillsets of economists and policymakers: its role in fostering sympathy and empathy. The poet, Percy Bysshe Shelley, underlined the role of imagination in sympathy and therefore morality in his *Defence of Poetry*:

> A man, to be greatly good, must imagine intensely and comprehensively; he must put himself in the place of another and of many others; the pains and pleasures of his species must become his own. The great instrument of the moral good is the imagination—and poetry administers to the effect by acting upon the cause.[21]

Such sympathetic identification with the plight of others is often seen as the quintessential opposite of the narrow self-interest of *homo economicus*. But care is needed with this simplistic view for several reasons. First, it's worth noting that the founder of modern economics, Adam Smith, was equally famous in his own day as the author of *The Theory of Moral Sentiments*, where he argued that susceptibility to the feelings of others and our ability to imagine ourselves in their predicament forms the basis of our moral judgments. Nothing in economics—the science of how markets behave—precludes us making judgments about how we *ought* to act to deliver particular non-market goals and help others.

Furthermore, our preferences as market participants—and even our sense of 'self'—are often extended laterally to include our desire to meet the needs and aspirations of those with whom we sympathise. Market preferences are very often for other-regarding and social goals, as companies chasing the green pound or dollar have clearly understood.

More iconoclastically still, the essayist William Hazlitt argued that the faculty of imaginative projection involved in sympathy with the feelings of others is fundamentally the same as that required to generate current interest in the future feelings of our own future selves. Indeed, in his hands, the quintessentially utilitarian conception of the pursuit of self-interest dissolves into an imaginative and creative enterprise: because the future is uncertain and even our identities and preferences change over time, we must imagine the interest that our imagined future selves would feel for an imagined future, and it is this imaginary that excites in us a current 'emotion of interest' sufficient to motivate us to act.[22] In other words, *homo economicus*—whether self-centred or altruistic—has no choice but to be a creature of the imagination, able to imagine what it will be like in a different time, place or version of self, if certain decisions are made, and then to act accordingly.

The ability to place ourselves in someone else's shoes and then stand back and judge how we want to behave can, of course, be the basis of market exploitation as well as moral restraint. Indeed, any entrepreneur or marketing agent has to imagine what it is like to be the client and then, armed with that empathic reading, judge how best to meet or exploit their preferences. Moreover, there is a wider sense in which empathy is the basis of good social science and good policymaking. As we have seen, market participants face a complex and multifaceted reality and an uncertain future that can always bear a number of different rational but inevitably partial and provisional interpretations. This means that, if we want to understand market behaviour or predict the impact of a novel policy or product offering, we have to interpret the contingent interpretations that others place on their predicament.

As a *social* science, economics cannot then escape the need to interpret a pre-interpreted world. And policymakers, too, must interpret the diverse ways in which economic actors visualise the present and imagine the uncertain future. This puts a premium on what the co-founder of the London School of Economics, Beatrice Webb, called 'analytical imagination'—the ability to project yourself into the contingent mindset of others and understand how they see the world.[23] At the same time, it explains the emphasis placed by governments on focus groups and by central banks on regional agencies that can access the narratives motivating the beliefs and actions of key players. It can also explain the recent explosion of interest in what Robert Shiller calls 'narrative economics'.[24] As he argues, many key inflection points in the economy reflect a sudden shift to a new dominant narrative. Among the most important of the real-time data that economists seeking to understand emerging trends must follow are sudden changes in the stories guiding investors and consumers.

In conclusion, let me draw together the three strands of a new more imaginative approach to economics, while summarising the lessons of Romantic epistemology—in particular, the ubiquity of uncertainty and the structuring role of models. In doing so, I will show ways in which these strands and lessons suggest that the *applied* use of economics in business or government is an art form rather than a mere exercise in calculating optimal policies on the basis of big data.

The first key lesson is that the constant drive on the part of business to design new products and novel methods, and on the part of governments for policy reform, imply that the economic future is radically uncertain. This means that entrepreneurs and policymakers alike must use economic and financial models, not as latter-day oracles for predicting the future, but as *diagnostic tools* for spotting emerging patterns.

The second key lesson is that all scientific theories, models, and metaphors are selective and focus only on certain aspects of a multi-faceted reality. Models and theories necessarily abstract from complexity to isolate and make sense of certain systematic tendencies. Their findings are presented with the caveat that 'other aspects' are assumed to 'remain equal' and can be safely ignored. But in the complex and uncertain world of modern capitalism—embedded as it is in plural societies and a global environment under stress—other things are rarely equal. As a result, the art of business or government requires *insight* into the interplay between the aspects of reality that are captured by different disciplines and models; and it requires *judgment* about how to balance those pools of knowledge with credible imaginaries about uncertain futures. Finally, it requires a combination of humility about how little is known with a willingness to constantly experiment with new metaphors and methods.

As we have seen, economists, entrepreneurs, and policymakers also need to learn to read the narratives, the stories, dreams and dystopias that motivate their fellow citizens, or might do so in future. In the fiendishly complex world of modern markets—and when faced with uncertain futures—we all have no choice but to *imagine* the future, *interpret* the creative interpretations that others place on their predicaments, and *invent* new ways of making sense of our own.

Endnotes

1 This paper is an edited transcript of a keynote address given at the inaugural convention of Platform Papers authors in July, 2021.

2 CP Snow, *The Two Cultures and the Scientific Revolution.* Cambridge University Press, 1959.

3 William Hazlitt, (1805), *An Essay on the Principles of Human Action.* Reprinted in *The Selected Writings of William Hazlitt.* Edited by Duncan Wu. Vol 1. Pickering and Chatto, 1998, pp.19–21.

4 Richard Bronk, *The Romantic Economist: Imagination in Economics.* Cambridge University Press, 2009.

5 David Fettig, Review of *The Romantic Economist*, in *Romanticism and Victorianism on the Net*, no. 56 (November 2009). https://doi.org/10.7202/1001110ar

6 Joseph Schumpeter (1943), *Capitalism, Socialism and Democracy.* Routledge, 1992, pp.83–84.

7 Jens Beckert, *Imagined Futures: Fictional Expectations and Capitalist Dynamics.* Harvard University Press, 2016, p.23.

8 Jens Beckert and Richard Bronk, 'An Introduction to Uncertain Futures' in *Uncertain Futures: Imaginaries, Narratives, and Calculation in the Economy*, edited by Jens Beckert and Richard Bronk. Oxford University Press, 2018

9 William Wordsworth, *The Prelude* (1805), Book XIII, line 98f. Edited by E de Selincourt. Oxford University Press, 1960, p.231.

10 John Stuart Mill (1873), *Autobiography.* Penguin, 1989, p.123.

11 Samuel Taylor Coleridge (1817), *Biographia Literaria*, Vol. 1, chapter XIII. Edited by J Shawcross. Oxford University Press, 1907, p.202.

12 William Wordsworth (1798), 'Lines Written a Few Miles above Tintern Abbey', line 106f, in *Lyrical Ballads*, reprinted in *Romanticism: An Anthology.* Edited by Duncan Wu. Blackwell, 1998, p.268; and The Prelude (1805), Book II, line 273, op. cit., p.27.

13 Samuel Taylor Coleridge (1830), *Table Talk*, 21 September. Reprinted in HJ Jackson, The Oxford Authors, *Samuel Taylor Coleridge*. Oxford University Press, 1985, p.596.

14 Kurt Heinzelman, *The Economics of the Imagination*. University of Massachusetts Press, 1980, p.9.

15 Deirdre N McCloskey, *The Rhetoric of Economics*. 2nd edn. University of Wisconsin Press, 1998.

16 Philip Mirowski, *More Heat than Light: Economics as Social Physics, Physics as Nature's Economics*. Cambridge University Press, 1989.

17 MH Abrams, *The Mirror and the Lamp: Romantic Theory and the Critical Tradition*. Oxford University Press, 1953, p.31.

18 Richard Bronk and Wade, Jacoby, 'Uncertainty and the Dangers of Monocultures in Regulation, Analysis and Practice', MPIfG Discussion Paper, 16/6, Max Planck Institute for the Study of Societies, 2016, 13. London School of Economics Research Online, e-print no. 66562.

19 Paul K Feyerabend, *Against Method*. 4th edn. Verso, 2010, p.20.

20 John Keats (1817), 'Letter to George and Tom Keats', 21 December. Extract reprinted in *Romanticism: An Anthology*. Edited by Duncan Wu, op. cit., p.1019.

21 Percy Bysshe Shelley (1840), *A Defence of Poetry*. Extract reprinted in *Romanticism: An Anthology*. Edited by Duncan Wu, op. cit., p.949.

22 William Hazlitt (1805), 'An Essay on the Principles of Human Action'. Reprinted in *The Selected Writings of William Hazlitt*. Edited by Duncan Wu. Vol. 1, op. cit., pp.12, 20f, 37; and see discussion in Richard Bronk, *The Romantic Economist*, op. cit., p.200.

23 Beatrice Webb, *My Apprenticeship* (1883). Extracts quoted and discussed in FR Leavis, 'Introduction', *Mill on Bentham and Coleridge*. Chatto & Windus, 1958, pp.24–26.

24 Robert J. Shiller, *Narrative Economics: How Stories Go Viral and Drive Major Economic Events*. Princeton University Press, 2019.

What's Wrong with Cannibalism?

Jonathan Biggins and John Quiggin
Awabakal and Worimi country / Turrbal and Jagera country

One of the key metaphors of economics is 'the invisible hand of the market' invented by Adam Smith. 'It is not from the benevolence of the butcher, the brewer, or the baker that we expect our dinner, but from their regard to their own self-interest,' he famously wrote in *The Wealth of Nations* in 1776. However, Smith was not the first to propose that market economies flourish through the pursuit of self-interest. The principle originated in satire. In 1705, Bernard Mandeville published a poem about a hive of bees who embraced consumerism and built a society of endless luxury:

> Thus Vice nurs'd Ingenuity,
> Which join'd with Time and Industry,

Had carry'd Life's Conveniencies,
It's real Pleasures, Comforts, Ease,
To such a Height, the very Poor
Liv'd better than the Rich before,
And nothing could be added more.

The Fable of the Bees takes the reader on a tour through the bees' metropolis, revealing corrupt behaviour in every institution. Eventually the bees tire of cheating each other and decide to reform, only to see their economy collapse. The whole swarm is last seen withdrawing inside a hollow log.

Jonathan Swift's essay *A Modest Proposal* was prompted by the British national debt crisis of 1729. Having offered conventional solutions in a number of essays, he turned to satire in frustration, proposing that landlords eat the children of their poor tenants:

> I grant this food will be somewhat dear, and therefore very proper for landlords, who, as they have already devoured most of the parents, seem to have the best title to the children ...

Modern economics originated in satire because its scenarios were a means of testing the principles of human social behaviour. If the principle was false, the scenario would turn to comedy. In the second session of day one of the Convention, we invited one of Australia's best-known political satirists, Jonathan Biggins, and one of its leading economists, John Quiggin, to discuss Mandeville and Swift's prophecies, with the convenor Harriet Parsons. Below is an edited version of their conversation.

JB: Good morning. Would you like to kick off, John?

JQ: Good question. Okay, I'll start. I'd like to acknowledge the traditional owners of the lovely land on which the lovely building you see behind you is based: the Turrbal and Jagera people in Brisbane.

Mandeville first. He presents an argument which certainly has not gone away: that human vices, primarily the vice of luxury and extravagance, contribute to general wellbeing. His argument very simply was, sure, everybody should live morally; but then what happens to all the luxury goods providers and all of the people who depend on them to keep the economy going? In *The Fable of the Bees*, the bees become incredibly rich, but eventually they get sick of immorality, so they reform and behave virtuously; but then they all end up in poverty. Essentially this is an argument for almost any kind of ill-advised public expenditure. That's a satirical version, of course. Adam Smith is a much deeper thinker than Mandeville and a more complex one than he's often portrayed. His other great work, *The Theory of Moral Sentiments*, cuts against this notion of unconstrained self-interest. His story in *The Wealth of Nations* only works in a society where people basically play by the rules and are motivated to act more or less honestly, within a legal structure that works for example. He's by no means the anarcho-capitalist some people suppose.

So how can this chaotic system, where everybody is just out for themselves, produce any kind of coherent outcome? The first answer to this question is that the price system does this. Everything else in economics is really just arguing about how well it does it. What else do we need to understand how individuals are acting? And also, what kind of social structures do we need, when the price system doesn't work?

JB: One of the interesting things about reading these two pieces is how little things have changed. I think the notion that not practising what you preach is what keeps the machinery of the economy going, is as true now as it was then. Swift's *A Modest Proposal* seems, yes, a ludicrous idea, but then look at Airbnb, where you monetise your family home. The home was the sacred hearth of the family. But then someone came up with the idea of selling part of it to strangers on a nightly basis. We recently toured to Orange in regional New South Wales. It has 364 Airbnbs, but no-one can rent a house there.

So you go back to *A Modest Proposal* and you can see the point: if you extend the rules of modern economics, you will get an outcome like that. At the same time, it's interesting the transfer of power that the tech revolution has made possible, out of the hands of the traditional guardians like the landed gentry etc, concentrating it in people like Jeff Bezos. The power is still there. It's just shifted it into different hands, and the hands are getting fewer and larger.

JQ: We've got a system of gatekeepers who have primarily set themselves up as ticket clippers. They may have different views about what they will allow or censor, but the essential job of the Zuckerbergs of this world is to say, 'You can have democratic access to information, but every time you look at it, you have to look at an ad.' They only receive a small amount for each ad, but, of course, if you have that monopoly, you can get big money. So the answer really is to do with institutions that favour monopolies and the way we've handled things like intellectual property. That has produced this particular subset of multi-billionaires.

JB: So how did economists fail to anticipate that there would be a swing back to unequal wealth?

JQ: The places where the big money is made has changed, but the real question isn't 'Why have these things happened?' It's 'Was something else possible?' Historically, with the exception of a few decades after 1945, and a distant past when nobody had anything, the world has always been divided into a tiny number of haves and a vast number of have-nots. That pattern was broken for the thirty years up to the 1970s, 'the Glorious Thirty' as the French call them. Inequality's now returned with a vengeance and that, in turn, has undermined a whole bunch of stories about how the economy works. Economists used to think there was a natural tendency for the economy to become more equal. First things would become more unequal, as the robber barons, the Vanderbilts and the Rockefellers, got rich. But then wealth would 'trickle down' or a 'rising tide would lift all boats' as society became more middle class. And, of course, that just hasn't happened.

The Keynesians, the dominant group of Keynesians anyway, had a fairly sophisticated but mechanical view of the world that thought of the economy as this complicated machine. That led to metaphors like 'fine tuning'; implying 'we can control it'. If you delve into science fiction, you come across so-called 'psycho-historians', social scientists who can plot out the future with high probability using statistical techniques. The economist Paul Krugman wrote somewhere in one of his columns that that's where he wanted to be: he didn't want to do economics. He wanted to be a psycho-historian. Bill Phillips built an 'analog computer' that would actually model the economy.

All that began failing in the late 60s and economists went into denial about the increasingly unequal distribution of wealth by saying, 'at least we still have lots of *opportunity*'. They believed they could keep on delivering the goods for the majority of people in the way that had been done in the post-war period.

Combine that with the financialisation of economics in the 1970s, when the Keynesian business model fell to bits, and it meant the finance sector was able to come along in the 1990s and say it could do a much better job. 'We've got these computers, we have these marvellous risk-reduction technologies. We can deliver prosperity. Just pay us immense sums of money and you will see the growth happen.' And for a while that seemed to be happening. Now it's not and we're seeing the reaction against Wall Street and Big Tech in the United States. Even fifteen years ago, both were viewed very favourably, by Democrats and Republicans alike. Now they see them as the enemy, but that's because of their immense power.

So nobody anticipated this happening. Now I think opinion has changed and faith in financialised economics has died. But nothing coherent has come to replace it.

JB: In some ways Facebook is Swiftian, in the sense of taking a theory or a proposal to its extreme. I mean, here is a system that was specifically designed to appeal to the addictive personality. And this is the stroke of genius: you don't realise its cumulative effect. The cumulative power. Taking it to its logical extension as the satirist would, we now see a system that will influence and alter democracy. It's not just altering the market. It's altering the political structures of most of the western world and the non-western world—the world.

JQ: Facebook created something which did a pretty good job of being addictive. But long before we worried about being addicted to the internet, people were sitting in front of the TV for hours on end, absorbing the same kind of ramped-up stuff. Or for that matter, listening to talkback radio. They both seem to do the job of hitting reinforcing stimuli pretty effectively. How that's done is a complicated story, but all social media has done is make things visible that were previously hard to see.

JB: Well, you could argue that Twitter is talkback radio with a much bigger switchboard.

But it's funny that these systems that were meant to create every colour of the rainbow—every shade of grey on the spectrum of opinion—have resulted in debate becoming black and white and now very few people can meet anywhere near the middle. Swift would be rolling in his grave at this: sixty per cent of the tweets in the US are generated by robots. Well, that's not a system that is human in scale, nor human in its effects.

You can compare it to the Luddites—who are much misunderstood. They saw the industrial revolution as a threat. And it was, as it did destroy their way of life. They weren't fearful of the technology. They were fearful of the social impact it was going to have on them. Now as it turned out, again, taking it to its logical conclusion, the industrial revolution has had many benefits, but the ultimate endgame is climate change. And the digital revolution is happening exponentially quicker than the industrial one.

Especially among arts practitioners and cultural institutions, the surrender to the digital has been swift and complete. At an artistic level, much of our cultural policy is now being dictated by social media platforms, and artists are increasingly self-censoring. We were recently told not to portray non-Caucasian characters in the Wharf Revue. We were portraying Xi Jinping and Kim Jong-un, two of the most powerful people in the world. I find it extraordinary that satirists are now being told who they can and can't offend. I would have thought the point was to offend everybody. If you deem it within your responsibility as a satirist, and you know where that boundary is drawn, you make that judgment. But now we're being told by management to hold back, before we even get to that point, because they are fearful of the backlash from the mob. You can arm a mob with pitchforks or iPads, they're still a mob. That's the inordinate effect social media is having on public debate, if you can have a debate any more.

JQ: It wasn't that long ago, certainly within my living memory, that you couldn't say the f-word.[1]

JB: Oh, yeah.

I guess you could look at the internet as a hive that is largely built on vice. I always find it interesting that the first website to make money was pornography. It still constitutes the greatest part of transactions on the internet. You look at things like TikTok and Instagram. Instagram started out with such high hopes. Certainly social media has been infiltrated and politicised to a point where the vices are way outweighing the virtues. Now, Mandeville would say, of course, well that's a good thing, because that keeps the whole thing bubbling along.

And, as we are talking about the price effect of culture, cultural policy is largely dictated now by people saying: 'Oh, you can bring two million dollars into the economy if you put the show on'. When you're doing a show, you see the restaurants around are full, and you know they're your audience, and you're supposed to think, 'Oh that's great. We're multiplying the economic effects.'

I know we should have grants, I know we should have monetary support for the arts. But I think the greatest support a government can give the arts is to put the arts on the agenda and give it the importance and the integrity that it deserves in public argument.

That's where Keating was quite good. Ironically, Labor governments have traditionally given less to the arts than Liberal governments, but he put it on the agenda, so it became not just a monetary thing. It became about the value and the importance of the sector. For me, the best way to support the arts is to find an audience that is willing to pay for it, and that's where I would rather we were. As a theatre practitioner, I'm just grateful that it works on the fairly straightforward principle that you pay for your ticket at the door, you come in, you see it, you go out and that's it. It will be the greatest irony of all if, when the digital revolution is over, the live performing arts are the only ones that can make any money. I look forward to that day.

JQ: I suppose it's important to remember that in a narrow sense the technological revolution helped build global finance, but most of this stuff was happening when the internet was still the province of starry-eyed idealists. It was government regulation and the law, not technology, that made the difference in terms of equity.

JB: I always found it interesting that the gig economy gained credibility because it was attached to an app, therefore in some way you were becoming self-employed. It's the way Howard successfully turned 'the battler' into 'the aspirational'. Once the working class was elevated to the middle class, they then became the natural constituents of the Liberal Party, because they were small business people. The same with the gig economy. But I look at the gig economy and I can see no difference to the hungry mile.

JQ: The gig economy, at least in the circles where I meet, is an entirely pejorative term. So, it comes down to your broader point about the Luddites. It's not the technology that does the damage but the interaction between the technology and society. There is no reason why the invention of a machine should make people worse off. Indeed, there was plenty of technological advancement in the glorious 30 years. Productivity grew massively and everybody benefitted, but people at the bottom benefitted more than the people at the top. The same should be true of current technology. It's the type of society that was created by the financial sector in the 1970s that has meant that things which should have been liberating are the opposite today.

If we go back to the nineteenth century, there's two kinds of artistic reactions to technological change. There's the Pre-Raphaelites with their 'let's turn our eyes away from terrible stuff and go back to painting pictures of Ophelia in the river', and there's Oscar Wilde and William Morris saying 'here's these machines; let's actually turn these brutal things into something liberating'. Let's not reject these tools. Let's make beautiful things with them. It seems to me that's the correct story. I don't want to prescribe for the arts, but there are opportunities to turn this around and to use it.

HP: I might ask a question here. We've been living out a dual narrative since the 1980s, where the government has been telling us that we're enjoying record economic growth, while for the arts the story has been austerity. 'The economy' seems to have become shorthand for the business economy. It hasn't taken into account government services or childcare, all those non-market-driven dimensions where the arts partially belong. Now the pandemic has thrown a spanner in the works by showing that you can close down the entire business economy—temporarily—so long as you've got social security, and can depend on the non-market-driven economy to ride out the crisis.

So what I'm thinking of is this: if the economy was a cake then in the past business was the cake and the non-market-driven economy was the icing on top. What the pandemic has done is flip that and say, 'no, it's the non-market-driven economy that's the cake and the business economy that is the icing.' What do you think about that as a metaphor?

JQ: I like it. Economists have spent a lot of time thinking about the household sector. It used to be possible to draw a boundary in agricultural economics between the household economy, which is where you sleep, and the productive economy, which is where you work with the pigs in the shed and the crops in the fields. What the pandemic has done is to show that the internet has broken down that boundary between the home and work and it makes no sense any more.

By the way, the guys who turn up on the TV talking about the movements of the stock market aren't economists. They're bank employees. So the focus on business is more reflective of the people employed by business as economists, rather than the people who actually do economics.

Among economists more generally, pro-market innovations really stopped a long time ago. The last big ideas were by people like Hayek and Friedman and they have been dead for a considerable time. We've seen their ideas being questioned. Alternative theories have been coming in for a long while.

In terms of the way people think about the pandemic, this is the third of three crises that have shifted things away from Hayek–Friedman. The first was the big dotcom bubble and bust in the 1990s. The financial markets did obviously crazy stuff and kept on doing it, and that undermined a lot of faith in the financial markets and the belief that they knew what they were doing. That faith was crushed again by the Global Financial Crisis in 2007. That time, governments came to the rescue. Then the advocates of austerity got back control and made an awful mess of things. As we've seen this time round, no-one has yet put their head up in any serious way to say that what we need now is austerity.

JB: As Richard Bronk mentioned in his opening remarks, the terms 'economy' and 'economists' are relatively recent. The bulk of the economy is what was once called 'life'. We need to rebrand the narrative, but it's very difficult. Malcolm Fraser once said politics shouldn't be on the front page of the newspaper. I agree with that, but everything is now political. It's like the culture wars. They only continue because it is in the interests of one side to continue the brand. As soon as they find a name or a label they can exploit, they leap onto it. If you want to talk about changing economic advice to government, or changing the way government formulates cultural policy, you have to find different labels.

HP: On that point I've got another metaphor. If it comes down to changing the language, we need to look at popular metaphors. What we're talking about now is, of course, 'the national debt' and how we can 'pay for it'. Economists have been wringing their hands over the metaphor that the federal government is like a household and it has to balance its budget.

JB: It's the *household* budget that has to be balanced. A federal budget never has to be balanced. Who remembers the Fraser/Howard deficit of '81? No-one!

JQ: It is the most bizarre metaphor. I mean, I can see twenty people here. I wouldn't be surprised if collectively we had $10 million of debt between us. As households. The idea that the government shouldn't borrow to buy stuff ... maybe my great-grandfather's household was like that. If we leave the debt to our grandchildren, we leave them our assets as well.

JB: How do we get to the point where the economic model is essentially a trickle up model?

JQ: This isn't the first time that people have been immensely rich. Carnegie and Rockefeller and Henry Ford got very, very rich. Henry Ford produced cars. We buy the cars and Henry Ford takes his bit off the top, pays the workers, pays the suppliers. All very straightforward. But when you look at the people who have got rich on the digital economy, and ask 'what is it that these people have actually done?' it's very hard to say. They seem to just have been in the right place at the right time, where a big stream of money was flying past. They're just scooping ladles of it out, having got in that position.

You can ask, 'what is Mark Zuckerberg producing?' We're doing all the work. All he's doing is collecting the data, which we let him collect, because we're unaware of it. He sells that data to somebody, who then uses it to sell us ads. There's no correspondence between contribution and return. The people who built the IP were basically university academics doing it in their spare time. They got nothing for it. It was people who came in and worked out a way to clip the tickets on the way through that have become rich. That, I think, is going to be the crucial factor in understanding how the social licence of the economy has been undermined.

HP: So is the universal basic income the answer for the arts?

JQ: I'm certainly a proponent of a version of the universal basic income, which is the level of income guarantee, which would include a basic living standard for artists engaged in creative work. It differs in the sense that you don't give it to Gina Rinehart and try to extract it back through taxes, you only expand the provision of basic incomes. But that would provide a basic income to anybody who wanted to apply themselves to creative work. That is something we could and should do.

HP: Could you explain how it works for those of us who haven't come across the idea?

JQ: Essentially it takes us back to the future. Let's say we go back to 1993, when the unemployment benefit was roughly the same as the age pension, something you could actually live on. Let's put that back in place, and instead of these incredibly onerous compliance conditions that assume that people are cheats and should be thrown out of the system, you say, we're going to *expand* what we consider to be a contribution to society, make it broader, and reflect the fact that we can afford to do this. That includes things like volunteering and creative work, potentially a grant for somebody setting up a small business, making it accessible to many more people. No radical change to the current system, but instead of Social Security finding a reason to throw people off unemployment benefits, you find something they can do, so they can stay on it, if they want to.

HP: National debt isn't a disaster. The pandemic has changed what it is possible to imagine by demonstrating that if you do pay people something approaching a universal basic income, in the form of JobKeeper, it actually creates economic growth.

Endnote

---

1 Fuck.

The Fable of the Bees or Private Vices, Publick Benefits

Bernard Mandeville (1670-1733)

Rotterdam, Dutch Republic, Hackney, Kingdom of Great Britain

A Spacious Hive well stockt with Bees,
That liv'd in Luxury and Ease;
And yet as fam'd for Laws and Arms,
As yielding large and early Swarms;
Was counted the great Nursery
Of Sciences and Industry.
No Bees had better Government,
More Fickleness, or less Content:
They were not Slaves to Tyranny,
Nor rul'd by wild Democracy;
But Kings, that could not wrong, because
Their Power was circumscrib'd by Laws.

THESE Insects liv'd like Men, and all
Our Actions they perform'd in small:
They did whatever's done in Town,
And what belongs to Sword or Gown:
Tho' th' Artful Works, by nimble Slight
Of minute Limbs, 'scap'd Human Sight;
Yet we've no Engines, Labourers,
Ships, Castles, Arms, Artificers,
Craft, Science, Shop, or Instrument,
But they had an Equivalent:
Which, since their Language is unknown,
Must be call'd, as we do our own.
As grant, that among other Things,
They wanted Dice, yet they had Kings;
And those had Guards; from whence we may
Justly conclude, they had some Play;
Unless a Regiment be shewn
Of Soldiers, that make use of none.

VAST Numbers throng'd the fruitful Hive;
Yet those vast Numbers made 'em thrive;
Millions endeavouring to supply
Each other's Lust and Vanity;
While other Millions were employ'd,
To see their Handy-works destroy'd;
They furnish'd half the Universe;
Yet had more Work than Labourers.
Some with vast Stocks, and little Pains,
Jump'd into Business of great Gains;
And some were damn'd to Sythes and Spades,
And all those hard laborious Trades;
Where willing Wretches daily sweat,
And wear out Strength and Limbs to eat:
While others follow'd Mysteries,
To which few Folks bind 'Prentices;
That want no Stock, but that of Brass,
And may set up without a Cross;
As Sharpers, Parasites, Pimps, Players,
Pick-pockets, Coiners, Quacks, South-sayers,
And all those, that in Enmity,
With downright Working, cunningly
Convert to their own Use the Labour
Of their good-natur'd heedless Neighbour.

These were call'd Knaves, but bar the Name,
The grave Industrious were the same:
All Trades and Places knew some Cheat,
No Calling was without Deceit.

THE *Lawyers, of whose Art the Basis*
Was raising Feuds and splitting Cases,
Oppos'd all Registers, that Cheats
Might make more Work with dipt Estates;
As wer't unlawful, that one's own,
Without a Law-Suit, should be known.
They kept off Hearings wilfully,
To finger the refreshing Fee;
And to defend a wicked Cause,
Examin'd and survey'd the Laws,
As Burglars Shops and Houses do,
To find out where they'd best break through.

PHYSICIANS *valu'd Fame and Wealth*
Above the drooping Patient's Health,
Or their own Skill: The greatest Part
Study'd, instead of Rules of Art,
Grave pensive Looks and dull Behaviour,
To gain th' Apothecary's Favour;
The Praise of Midwives, Priests, and all
That serv'd at Birth or Funeral.
To bear with th' ever-talking Tribe,
And hear my Lady's Aunt prescribe;
With formal Smile, and kind How d'ye,
To fawn on all the Family;
And, which of all the greatest Curse is,
T' endure th' Impertinence of Nurses.

AMONG *the many Priests of* Jove,
Hir'd to draw Blessings from Above,
Some few were Learn'd and Eloquent,
But thousands Hot and Ignorant:
Yet all pass'd Muster that could hide
Their Sloth, Lust, Avarice and Pride;
For which they were as fam'd as Tailors
For Cabbage, or for Brandy Sailors:
Some, meagre-look'd, and meanly clad,
Would mystically pray for Bread,
Meaning by that an ample Store,
Yet lit'rally received no more;
And, while these holy Drudges starv'd,
The lazy Ones, for which they serv'd,
Indulg'd their Ease, with all the Graces
Of Health and Plenty in their Faces.

THE *Soldiers, that were forc'd to fight,*
If they surviv'd, got Honour by't;
Tho' some, that shunn'd the bloody Fray,
Had Limbs shot off, that ran away:
Some valiant Gen'rals fought the Foe;
Others took Bribes to let them go:
Some ventur'd always where 'twas warm,
Lost now a Leg, and then an Arm;
Till quite disabled, and put by,
They liv'd on half their Salary;
While others never came in Play,
And staid at Home for double Pay.

THEIR *Kings were serv'd, but Knavishly,*
Cheated by their own Ministry;
Many, that for their Welfare slaved,
Robbing the very Crown they saved:
Pensions were small, and they liv'd high,
Yet boasted of their Honesty.
Calling, whene'er they strain'd their Right,
The slipp'ry Trick a Perquisite;
And when Folks understood their Cant,
They chang'd that for Emolument;
Unwilling to be short or plain,
In any thing concerning Gain;
For there was not a Bee but would

Get more, I won't say, than he should;
But than he dar'd to let them know,
That pay'd for't; as your Gamesters do,
That, tho' at fair Play, ne'er will own
Before the Losers what they've won.

But who can all their Frauds repeat?
The very Stuff, which in the Street
They sold for Dirt t'enrich the Ground,
Was often by the Buyers found
Sophisticated with a quarter
Of good-for-nothing Stones and Mortar;
Tho' Flail *had little Cause to mutter,*
Who sold the other Salt for Butter.

Justice her self, fam'd for fair Dealing,
By Blindness had not lost her Feeling;
Her Left Hand, which the Scales should hold,
Had often dropt 'em, brib'd with Gold;
And, tho' she seem'd Impartial,
Where Punishment was corporal,
Pretended to a reg'lar Course,
In Murther, and all Crimes of Force;
Tho' some, first pillory'd for Cheating,
Were hang'd in Hemp of their own beating;
Yet, it was thought, the Sword she bore
Check'd but the Desp'rate and the Poor;
That, urg'd by meer Necessity,
Were ty'd up to the wretched Tree
For Crimes, which not deserv'd that Fate,
But to secure the Rich and Great.

Thus every Part was full of Vice,
Yet the whole Mass a Paradise;
Flatter'd in Peace, and fear'd in Wars,
They were th' Esteem of Foreigners,
And lavish of their Wealth and Lives,
The Balance of all other Hives.
Such were the Blessings of that State;
Their Crimes conspir'd to make them Great:
And Virtue, who from Politicks
Had learn'd a Thousand Cunning Tricks,
Was, by their happy Influence,
Made Friends with Vice: And ever since,
The worst of all the Multitude
Did something for the Common Good.

This was the States Craft, that maintain'd
The Whole of which each Part complain'd:
This, as in Musick Harmony,
Made Jarrings in the main agree;
Parties directly opposite,
Assist each other, as 'twere for Spight;
And Temp'rance with Sobriety,
Serve Drunkenness and Gluttony.

The Root of Evil, Avarice,
That damn'd ill-natur'd baneful Vice,
Was Slave to Prodigality,
That noble Sin; whilst Luxury
Employ'd a Million of the Poor,
And odious Pride a Million more:
Envy it self, and Vanity,
Were Ministers of Industry;
Their darling Folly, Fickleness,
In Diet, Furniture and Dress,
That strange ridic'lous Vice, was made
The very Wheel that turn'd the Trade.
Their Laws and Clothes were equally
Objects of Mutability;
For, what was well done for a time,
In half a Year became a Crime;
Yet while they alter'd thus their Laws,

Still finding and correcting Flaws,
They mended by Inconstancy
Faults, which no Prudence could foresee.

THUS Vice nurs'd Ingenuity,
Which join'd with Time and Industry,
Had carry'd Life's Conveniencies,
It's real Pleasures, Comforts, Ease,
To such a Height, the very Poor
Liv'd better than the Rich before,
And nothing could be added more.

HOW Vain is Mortal Happiness!
Had they but known the Bounds of Bliss;
And that Perfection here below
Is more than Gods can well bestow;
The Grumbling Brutes had been content
With Ministers and Government.
But they, at every ill Success,
Like Creatures lost without Redress,
Curs'd Politicians, Armies, Fleets;
While every one cry'd, Damn the Cheats,
And would, tho' conscious of his own,
In others barb'rously bear none.

ONE, that had got a Princely Store,
By cheating Master, King and Poor,
Dar'd cry aloud, The Land must sink
For all its Fraud; *And whom d'ye think*
The Sermonizing Rascal chid?
A Glover that sold Lamb for Kid.

THE least thing was not done amiss,
Or cross'd the Publick Business;
But all the Rogues cry'd brazenly,
Good Gods, Had we but Honesty!
Merc'ry *smil'd at th' Impudence,*
And others call'd it want of Sense,
Always to rail at what they lov'd:
But Jove *with Indignation mov'd,*
At last in Anger swore, He'd rid
The bawling Hive of Fraud; *and did.*
The very Moment it departs,
And Honesty fills all their Hearts;
There shews 'em, like th' Instructive Tree,
Those Crimes which they're asham'd to see;
Which now in Silence they confess,
By blushing at their Ugliness:
Like Children, that would hide their Faults,
And by their Colour own their Thoughts:
Imag'ning, when they're look'd upon,
That others see what they have done.

BUT, Oh ye Gods! What Consternation,
How vast and sudden was th' Alteration!
In half an Hour, the Nation round,
Meat fell a Peny in the Pound.
The Mask Hypocrisy's flung down,
From the great Statesman to the Clown:
And some in borrow'd Looks well known,
Appear'd like Strangers in their own.
The Bar was silent from that Day;
For now the willing Debtors pay,
Ev'n what's by Creditors forgot;
Who quitted them that had it not.
Those, that were in the Wrong, stood mute,
And dropt the patch'd vexatious Suit:
On which since nothing less can thrive,
Than Lawyers in an honest Hive,
All, except those that got enough,
With Inkhorns by their sides troop'd off.

JUSTICE hang'd some, set others free;
And after Goal delivery,
Her Presence being no more requir'd,

With all her Train and Pomp retir'd.
First march'd some Smiths with Locks and Grates,
Fetters, and Doors with Iron Plates:
Next Goalers, Turnkeys and Assistants:
Before the Goddess, at some distance,
Her chief and faithful Minister,
'Squire CATCH, *the Law's great Finisher,*
Bore not th' imaginary Sword,
But his own Tools, an Ax and Cord:
Then on a Cloud the Hood-wink'd Fair,
JUSTICE *her self was push'd by Air:*
About her Chariot, and behind,
Were Serjeants, Bums of every kind,
Tip-staffs, and all those Officers,
That squeeze a Living out of Tears.

THO' *Physick liv'd, while Folks were ill,*
None would prescribe, but Bees of skill,
Which through the Hive dispers'd so wide,
That none of them had need to ride;
Wav'd vain Disputes, and strove to free
The Patients of their Misery;
Left Drugs in cheating Countries grown,
And us'd the Product of their own;
Knowing the Gods sent no Disease
To Nations without Remedies.

THEIR *Clergy rous'd from Laziness,*
Laid not their Charge on Journey-Bees;
But serv'd themselves, exempt from Vice,
The Gods with Pray'r and Sacrifice;
All those, that were unfit, or knew
Their Service might be spar'd, withdrew:
Nor was there Business for so many,
(If th' Honest stand in need of any,)
Few only with the High-Priest staid,
To whom the rest Obedience paid:
Himself employ'd in Holy Cares,
Resign'd to others State-Affairs.
He chas'd no Starv'ling from his Door,
Nor pinch'd the Wages of the Poor;
But at his House the Hungry's fed,
The Hireling finds unmeasur'd Bread,
The needy Trav'ler Board and Bed.

AMONG *the King's great Ministers,*
And all th' inferior Officers
The Change was great; for frugally
They now liv'd on their Salary:
That a poor Bee should ten times come
To ask his Due, a trifling Sum,
And by some well-hir'd Clerk be made
To give a Crown, or ne'er be paid,
Would now be call'd a downright Cheat,
Tho' formerly a Perquisite.
All Places manag'd first by Three,
Who watch'd each other's Knavery,
And often for a Fellow-feeling,
Promoted one another's stealing,
Are happily supply'd by One,
By which some thousands more are gone.

NO *Honour now could be content,*
To live and owe for what was spent;
Liv'ries in Brokers Shops are hung,
They part with Coaches for a Song;
Sell stately Horses by whole Sets;
And Country-Houses, to pay Debts.

VAIN *Cost is shunn'd as much as Fraud;*
They have no Forces kept Abroad;
Laugh at th' Esteem of Foreigners,
And empty Glory got by Wars;
They fight, but for their Country's sake,
When Right or Liberty's at Stake.

NOW *mind the glorious Hive, and see*
How Honesty and Trade agree.

The Shew is gone, it thins apace;
And looks with quite another Face.
For 'twas not only that They went,
By whom vast Sums were Yearly spent;
But Multitudes that liv'd on them,
Were daily forc'd to do the same.
In vain to other Trades they'd fly;
All were o'er-stock'd accordingly.

The Price of Land and Houses falls;
Mirac'lous Palaces, whose Walls,
Like those of Thebes, *were rais'd by Play,*
Are to be let; while the once gay,
Well-seated Houshold Gods would be
More pleas'd to expire in Flames, than see
The mean Inscription on the Door
Smile at the lofty ones they bore.
The building Trade is quite destroy'd,
Artificers are not employ'd;
No Limner for his Art is fam'd,
Stone-cutters, Carvers are not nam'd.

Those, that remain'd, grown temp'rate, strive,
Not how to spend, but how to live,
And, when they paid their Tavern Score,
Resolv'd to enter it no more:
No Vintner's Jilt in all the Hive
Could wear now Cloth of Gold, and thrive;
Nor Torcol *such vast Sums advance,*
For Burgundy *and* Ortelans*;*
The Courtier's gone, that with his Miss
Supp'd at his House on Christmas *Peas;*
Spending as much in two Hours stay,
As keeps a Troop of Horse a Day.

The haughty Chloe, to live Great,
Had made her Husband rob the State:
But now she sells her Furniture,
Which th' Indies *had been ransack'd for;*
Contracts th' expensive Bill of Fare,
And wears her strong Suit a whole Year:
The slight and fickle Age is past;
And Clothes, as well as Fashions, last.
Weavers, that join'd rich Silk with Plate,
And all the Trades subordinate,
Are gone. Still Peace and Plenty reign,
And every Thing is cheap, tho' plain:
Kind Nature, free from Gard'ners Force,
Allows all Fruits in her own Course;
But Rarities cannot be had,
Where Pains to get them are not paid.

As Pride and Luxury decrease,
So by degrees they leave the Seas.
Not Merchants now, but Companies
Remove whole Manufactories.
All Arts and Crafts neglected lie;
Content, the Bane of Industry,
Makes 'em admire their homely Store,
And neither seek nor covet more.

So few in the vast Hive remain,
The hundredth Part they can't maintain
Against th' Insults of numerous Foes;
Whom yet they valiantly oppose:
'Till some well-fenc'd Retreat is found,
And here they die or stand their Ground.
No Hireling in their Army's known;
But bravely fighting for their own,
Their Courage and Integrity
At last were crown'd with Victory.
They triumph'd not without their Cost,
For many Thousand Bees were lost.
Hard'ned with Toils and Exercise,
They counted Ease it self a Vice;
Which so improv'd their Temperance;
That, to avoid Extravagance,

They flew into a hollow Tree,
Blest with Content and Honesty.

THE MORAL

THEN leave Complaints: Fools only strive
To make a Great an Honest Hive
T' enjoy the World's Conveniencies,
Be fam'd in War, yet live in Ease,
Without great Vices, is a vain
EUTOPIA seated in the Brain.
Fraud, Luxury and Pride must live,
While we the Benefits receive:
Hunger's a dreadful Plague, no doubt,
Yet who digests or thrives without?
Do we not owe the Growth of Wine
To the dry shabby crooked Vine?
Which, while its Shoots neglected stood,
Chok'd other Plants, and ran to Wood;
But blest us with its noble Fruit,
As soon as it was ty'd and cut:
So Vice is beneficial found,
When it's by Justice lopt and bound;
Nay, where the People would be great,
As necessary to the State,
As Hunger is to make 'em eat.
Bare Virtue can't make Nations live
In Splendor; they, that would revive
A Golden Age, must be as free,
For Acorns, as for Honesty.

FINIS

A Modest Proposal for preventing the children of poor people in Ireland, from being a burden on their parents or country, and for making them beneficial to the publick.

Jonathan Swift (1667–1745)
Dublin, Ireland

It is a melancholy object to those, who walk through this great town, or travel in the country, when they see the streets, the roads, and cabbin-doors crowded with beggars of the female sex, followed by three, four, or six children, all in rags, and importuning every passenger for an alms. These mothers, instead of being able to work for their honest livelihood, are forced to employ all their time in strolling to beg sustenance for their helpless infants who, as they grow up, either turn thieves for want of work, or leave their dear native country, to fight for the Pretender in Spain, or sell themselves to the Barbadoes.

I think it is agreed by all parties, that this prodigious number of children in the arms, or on the backs, or at the heels of their mothers, and frequently of their fathers, is in the present deplorable state of the kingdom, a very great additional grievance; and therefore whoever could find out a fair, cheap and easy method of making these children sound and useful members of the commonwealth, would deserve so well of the publick, as to have his statue set up for a preserver of the nation.

But my intention is very far from being confined to provide only for the children of professed beggars: it is of a much greater extent, and shall take in the whole number of infants at a certain age, who are born of parents in effect as little able to support them, as those who demand our charity in the streets.

As to my own part, having turned my thoughts for many years upon this important subject, and maturely weighed the several schemes of our projectors, I have always found them grossly mistaken in their computation. It is true, a child just dropt from its dam, may be supported by her milk, for a solar year, with little other nourishment: at most not above the value of two shillings, which the mother may certainly get, or the value in scraps, by her lawful occupation of begging; and it is exactly at one year old that I propose to provide for them in such a manner, as, instead of being a charge upon their parents, or the parish, or wanting food and raiment for the rest of their lives, they shall, on the contrary, contribute to the feeding, and partly to the clothing of many thousands.

There is likewise another great advantage in my scheme, that it will prevent those voluntary abortions, and that horrid practice of women murdering their bastard children, alas! too frequent among us, sacrificing the poor innocent babes, I doubt, more to avoid the expence than the shame, which would move tears and pity in the most savage and inhuman breast.

The number of souls in this kingdom being usually reckoned one million and a half, of these I calculate there may be about two hundred thousand couple, whose wives are breeders; from which number I subtract thirty thousand couple, who are able to maintain their own children, (although I apprehend there cannot be so many under the present distresses of the kingdom) but this being granted, there will remain a hundred and seventy thousand breeders. I again subtract fifty thousand, for those women who miscarry, or whose children die by accident or disease within the year. There only remain a hundred and twenty thousand children of poor parents annually born. The question therefore is, How this number shall be reared and provided for? which, as I have already said, under the present situation of affairs, is utterly impossible by all the methods hitherto proposed. For we can neither employ them in handicraft or agriculture; they neither build houses, (I mean in the country) nor cultivate land: they can very seldom pick up a livelihood by stealing till they arrive at six years old; except where they are of towardly parts, although I confess they learn the rudiments much earlier; during which time they can however be properly looked upon only as probationers; as I have been informed by a principal gentleman in the county of Cavan, who protested to me, that he never knew above one or two instances under the age of six, even in a part of the kingdom so renowned for the quickest proficiency in that art.

I am assured by our merchants, that a boy or a girl, before twelve years old, is no saleable commodity, and even when they come to this age, they will not yield above three pounds, or three pounds and half a crown at most, on the exchange; which cannot turn to account either to the parents or kingdom, the charge of nutriments and rags having been at least four times that value.

I shall now therefore humbly propose my own thoughts, which I hope will not be liable to the least objection.

I have been assured by a very knowing American of my acquaintance in London, that a young healthy child well nursed, is, at a year old, a most delicious nourishing and wholesome food, whether stewed, roasted, baked, or boiled; and I make no doubt that it will equally serve in a fricasee, or a ragoust.

I do therefore humbly offer it to publick consideration, that of the hundred and twenty thousand children, already computed, twenty thousand may be reserved for breed, whereof only one fourth part to be males; which is more than we allow to sheep, black cattle, or swine, and my reason is, that these children are seldom the fruits of marriage, a circumstance not much regarded by our savages, therefore, one male will be sufficient to serve four females. That the remaining hundred thousand may, at a year old, be offered in sale to the persons of quality and fortune, through the kingdom, always advising the mother to let them suck plentifully in the last month, so as to render them plump, and fat for a good table. A child will make two dishes at an entertainment for friends, and when the family dines alone, the fore or hind quarter will make a reasonable dish, and seasoned with a little pepper or salt, will be very good boiled on the fourth day, especially in winter.

I have reckoned upon a medium, that a child just born will weigh 12 pounds, and in a solar year, if tolerably nursed, encreaseth to 28 pounds.

I grant this food will be somewhat dear, and therefore very proper for landlords, who, as they have already devoured most of the parents, seem to have the best title to the children.

Infant's flesh will be in season throughout the year, but more plentiful in March, and a little before and after; for we are told by a grave author, an eminent French physician, that fish being a prolifick dyet, there are more children born in Roman Catholick countries about nine months after Lent, than at any other season; therefore, reckoning a year after Lent, the markets will be more glutted than usual, because the number of Popish infants, is at least three to one in this kingdom, and therefore it will have one other collateral advantage, by lessening the number of Papists among us.

I have already computed the charge of nursing a beggar's child (in which list I reckon all cottagers, labourers, and four-fifths of the farmers) to be about two shillings per annum, rags included; and I believe no gentleman would repine to give ten shillings for the carcass of a good fat child, which, as I have said, will make four dishes of excellent nutritive meat, when he hath only some particular friend, or his own family to dine with him. Thus the squire will learn to be a good landlord, and grow popular among his tenants, the mother will have eight shillings neat profit, and be fit for work till she produces another child.

Those who are more thrifty (as I must confess the times require) may flay the carcass; the skin of which, artificially dressed, will make admirable gloves for ladies, and summer boots for fine gentlemen.

As to our City of Dublin, shambles may be appointed for this purpose, in the most convenient parts of it, and butchers we may be assured will not be wanting; although I rather recommend buying the children alive, and dressing them hot from the knife, as we do roasting pigs.

A very worthy person, a true lover of his country, and whose virtues I highly esteem, was lately pleased in discoursing on this matter, to offer a refinement upon my scheme. He said, that many gentlemen of this kingdom, having of late destroyed their deer, he conceived that the want of venison might be well supplied by the bodies of young lads and maidens, not exceeding fourteen years of age, nor under twelve; so great a number of both sexes in every county being now ready to starve for want of work and service: and these to be disposed of by their parents if alive, or otherwise by their nearest relations. But with due deference to so excellent a friend, and so deserving a patriot, I cannot be altogether in his sentiments; for as to the males, my American acquaintance assured me from frequent experience, that their flesh was generally tough and lean, like that of our schoolboys, by continual exercise, and their taste disagreeable, and to fatten them would not answer the charge. Then as to the females, it would, I think, with humble submission, be a loss to the publick, because they soon would become breeders themselves: and besides, it is not improbable that some scrupulous people might be apt to censure such a practice, (although indeed very unjustly) as a little bordering upon cruelty, which, I confess, hath always been with me the strongest objection against any project, how well soever intended.

But in order to justify my friend, he confessed, that this expedient was put into his head by the famous Psalmanaazor, a native of the island Formosa, who came from thence to London, above twenty years ago, and in conversation told my friend, that in his country, when any young person happened to be put to death, the executioner sold the carcass to persons of quality, as a prime dainty; and that, in his time, the body of a plump girl of fifteen, who was crucified for an attempt to poison the Emperor, was sold to his imperial majesty's prime minister of state, and other great mandarins of the court in joints from the gibbet, at four hundred crowns. Neither indeed can I deny, that if the same use were made of several plump young girls in this town, who without one single groat to their fortunes, cannot stir abroad without a chair, and appear at a playhouse and assemblies in foreign fineries which they never will pay for, the kingdom would not be the worse.

Some persons of a desponding spirit are in great concern about that vast number of poor people, who are aged, diseased, or maimed; and I have been desired to employ my thoughts what course may be taken, to ease the nation of so grievous an incumbrance. But I am not in the least pain upon that matter, because it is very well known, that they are every day dying, and rotting, by cold and famine, and filth, and vermin, as fast as can be reasonably expected. And as to the young labourers, they are now in almost as hopeful a condition. They cannot get work, and consequently pine away from want of nourishment, to a degree, that if at any time they are accidentally hired to common labour, they have not strength to perform it, and thus the country and themselves are happily delivered from the evils to come.

I have too long digressed, and therefore shall return to my subject. I think the advantages by the proposal which I have made are obvious and many, as well as of the highest importance.

For first, as I have already observed, it would greatly lessen the number of Papists, with whom we are yearly overrun, being the principal breeders of the nation, as well as our most dangerous enemies, and who stay at home on purpose with a design to deliver the kingdom to the Pretender, hoping to take their advantage by the absence of so many good Protestants, who have chosen rather to leave their country, than stay at home and pay tithes against their conscience to an episcopal curate.

Secondly, The poorer tenants will have something valuable of their own, which by law may be made liable to a distress, and help to pay their landlord's rent, their corn and cattle being already seized, and money a thing unknown.

Thirdly, Whereas the maintainance of a hundred thousand children, from two years old, and upwards, cannot be computed at less than ten shillings a piece per annum, the nation's stock will be thereby encreased fifty thousand pounds per annum, besides the profit of a new dish, introduced to the tables of all gentlemen of fortune in the kingdom, who have any refinement in taste. And the money will circulate among our selves, the goods being entirely of our own growth and manufacture.

Fourthly, The constant breeders, besides the gain of eight shillings sterling per annum by the sale of their children, will be rid of the charge of maintaining them after the first year.

Fifthly, This food would likewise bring great custom to taverns, where the vintners will certainly be so prudent as to procure the best receipts for dressing it to perfection; and consequently have their houses frequented by all the fine gentlemen, who justly value themselves upon their knowledge in good eating; and a skilful cook, who understands how to oblige his guests, will contrive to make it as expensive as they please.

Sixthly, This would be a great inducement to marriage, which all wise nations have either encouraged by rewards, or enforced by laws and penalties. It would encrease the care and tenderness of mothers towards their children, when they were sure of a settlement for life to the poor babes, provided in some sort by the publick, to their annual profit instead of expence. We should soon see an honest emulation among the married women, which of them could bring the fattest child to the market. Men would become as fond of their wives, during the time of their pregnancy, as they are now of their mares in foal, their cows in calf, or sows when they are ready to farrow; nor offer to beat or kick them (as is too frequent a practice) for fear of a miscarriage.

Many other advantages might be enumerated. For instance, the addition of some thousand carcasses in our exportation of barrel'd beef: the propagation of swine's flesh, and improvement in the art of making good bacon, so much wanted among us by the great destruction of pigs, too frequent at our tables; which are no way comparable in taste or magnificence to a well grown, fat yearling child, which roasted whole will make a considerable figure at a Lord Mayor's feast, or any other publick entertainment. But this, and many others, I omit, being studious of brevity.

Supposing that one thousand families in this city, would be constant customers for infants flesh, besides others who might have it at merry meetings, particularly at weddings and christenings, I compute that Dublin would take off annually about twenty thousand carcasses; and the rest of the kingdom (where probably they will be sold somewhat cheaper) the remaining eighty thousand.

I can think of no one objection, that will possibly be raised against this proposal, unless it should be urged, that the number of people will be thereby much lessened in the kingdom. This I freely own, and it was indeed one principal design in offering it to the world. I desire the reader will observe, that I calculate my remedy for this one individual Kingdom of Ireland, and for no other that ever was, is, or, I think, ever can be upon Earth. Therefore let no man talk to me of other expedients: Of taxing our absentees at five shillings a pound: Of using neither clothes, nor houshold furniture, except what is of our own growth and manufacture: Of utterly rejecting the materials and instruments that promote foreign luxury: Of curing the expensiveness of pride, vanity, idleness, and gaming in our women: Of introducing a vein of parsimony, prudence and temperance: Of learning to love our country, wherein we differ even from Laplanders, and the inhabitants of Topinamboo: Of quitting our animosities and factions, nor acting any longer like the Jews, who were murdering one another at the very moment their city was taken: Of being a little cautious not to sell our country and consciences for nothing: Of teaching landlords to have at least one degree of mercy towards their tenants. Lastly, of putting a spirit of honesty, industry, and skill into our shopkeepers, who, if a resolution could now be taken to buy only our native goods, would immediately unite to cheat and exact upon us in the price, the measure, and the goodness, nor could ever yet be brought to make one fair proposal of just dealing, though often and earnestly invited to it.

Therefore I repeat, let no man talk to me of these and the like expedients, till he hath at least some glympse of hope, that there will ever be some hearty and sincere attempt to put them into practice.

But, as to myself, having been wearied out for many years with offering vain, idle, visionary thoughts, and at length utterly despairing of success, I fortunately fell upon this proposal, which, as it is wholly new, so it hath something solid and real, of no expence and little trouble, full in our own power, and whereby we can incur no danger in disobliging England. For this kind of commodity will not bear exportation, and flesh being of too tender a consistence, to admit a long continuance in salt, although perhaps I could name a country, which would be glad to eat up our whole nation without it.

After all, I am not so violently bent upon my own opinion, as to reject any offer, proposed by wise men, which shall be found equally innocent, cheap, easy, and effectual. But before something of that kind shall be advanced in contradiction to my scheme, and offering a better, I desire the author or authors will be pleased maturely to consider two points. First, As things now stand, how they will be able to find food and raiment for a hundred thousand useless mouths and backs. And secondly, There being a round million of creatures in human figure throughout this kingdom, whose whole subsistence put into a common stock, would leave them in debt two million of pounds sterling, adding those who are beggars by profession, to the bulk of farmers, cottagers and labourers, with their wives and children, who are beggars in effect; I desire those politicians who dislike my overture, and may perhaps be so bold to attempt an answer, that they will first ask the parents of these mortals, whether they would not at this day think it a great happiness to have been sold for food at a year old, in the manner I prescribe, and thereby have avoided such a perpetual scene of misfortunes, as they have since gone through, by the oppression of landlords, the impossibility of paying rent without money or trade, the want of common sustenance, with neither house nor clothes to cover them from the inclemencies of the weather, and the most inevitable prospect of intailing the like, or greater miseries, upon their breed for ever.

I profess in the sincerity of my heart, that I have not the least personal interest in endeavouring to promote this necessary work, having no other motive than the publick good of my country, by advancing our trade, providing for infants, relieving the poor, and giving some pleasure to the rich. I have no children, by which I can propose to get a single penny; the youngest being nine years old, and my wife past child-bearing.

You Can Sing (Averagely)!

Astrid Jorgensen
Turrbal and Jagera country

You can sing.

Probably not amazingly, but most certainly, you can sing. If you have the ability to speak, the same vocal mechanisms you use gossiping at work, or yelling at the footy, or having a lockdown cry, are the ones that will allow you, if you wanted, to sing a Puccini aria.

True, you might be spectacularly far from stage-ready, but there is a very real, persistent belief out there that if you can't sing well first go, you are doomed to sing badly forever. You may say, 'Oh, I can't sing, I'm absolutely tone deaf,' despite the fact that the medical occurrence of the clinical disorder of amusia, or true tone deafness, affects only four per cent of the population.

Congenital amusia—usually as a result of brain damage—is an inability to recognise familiar melodies. If you enjoy listening to music, you are not tone deaf, not even close.

Perhaps you do sing out of tune. But if your only singing training has consisted of yelling songs in your car while stuck in traffic, what did you expect? Do you refuse to cook food because you won't win a Michelin star? Do you refuse to exercise because you aren't on track for an Olympic Gold? Somewhere along the way we've become convinced that we can only ever be bystanders and consumers of music. I implore you to reconsider.

Receiving my first singing lesson when I was 16 felt like receiving instructions to a magic spell which I could cast over others simply by singing at them. That I could use my body as an instrument to create sounds that made people feel complicated emotions was an astounding revelation. I knew then that I wanted to teach people to sing so that they could experience this phenomenon for themselves.

I started with high-school teaching. In 2011, I landed my first job at a prestigious school in Brisbane. Every lesson saw me bounce into the classroom, a *Sister Act 2 (Back In the Habit)*-style lesson plan clasped in my sweaty hands, ready for my movie montage where I would transform a ragtag class of misfits into the All State Champion choir (I will never be sorry for the specificity of this 1993 reference). Mostly, I ended up crying in my car on the way home. After the first year, I only taught in reluctant, contractual bursts.

I could not wrap my head around the fact that teenagers were spending every second of their lives consumed by music while simultaneously proclaiming to hate Music, the subject. They would walk into the classroom with their favourite singer blasting in their headphones, then take the headphones out, slump in their chair and despise singing with me for 50 minutes. I started to worry that I was ruining music-making for children, which was a heavy burden to bear.

One available interpretation was that I was simply a terrible, inexperienced teacher. Perhaps this was a contributing factor! But even in my most self-deprecating moods I knew there were other reasons.

Teaching music is a unique challenge because our experience of music is fluidly woven into the fabric of our lives. We're all musical experts in our own way. We hear music at the shops, in movies, in our rideshares, at a funeral—the list goes on. We use music to lock in pivotal memories throughout our lives. We curate playlists to suit our every mood. Music makes us feel connected. It can make us feel, full stop. But to create music requires us to unpick all that, to take what was a fluid experience and make it static. For most of us there is a chasm between what we love to listen to and what we can personally do. This feeling of inadequacy is heightened when (you think) you can't sing 'well'. It's more personal because you make the bad noises with your own body.

Unsure how to solve the issue of experiential fluidity in the classroom, I scurried out of schools and into the community choir space. By 2017 I was directing seven separate choirs and driving hundreds of kilometres each week to sing with as many people as possible. It was an exhausting, exhilarating ride, and I finally felt free to share my love of singing with like-minded, enthusiastic individuals. Directing choirs allowed me to curate fluid musical experiences for small groups of singers where they made beautiful art just by sharing their voices.

But there was one thing still bothering me. None of these choirs reflected me in any way. Each of my seven choirs were either made up of kids forced to sing by their parents, or were mostly white, semi-retirees. There is nothing unpleasant about working with either group. But as a 20-something Asian woman myself, it was confusing to me that none of my peers wanted to sing.

So in 2017, after years of friends declining to sing with me, I wrote a list. On it, I put every excuse I'd ever heard about what stopped somebody from joining a choir:

Auditions
Time commitment
Having to compete/perform
Reading sheet music
Unfamiliar repertoire
General choir lameness
Having a bad singing voice.

I determined to solve all of these roadblocks. Thus, Pub Choir was born.

Not always in a pub, the trademarked name, Pub Choir, describes my musical act. It's a ticketed show during which I transform an audience—any audience—into a functional choir. When you buy a ticket to Pub Choir, you agree to become a chorister for an evening, with me as your choirmaster. By the end of the show, my accompanist Waveney Yasso and I become your audience of two, while you and your (sometimes thousands of) fellow singers perform what you have learned—usually a well-known pop song—in three-part harmony.

In 2019, I taught around 57,000 people at various Pub Choir events around the world. Pub Choir has collaborated with the likes of Paul Kelly, Ben Lee, Meg Mac and the Queensland Symphony Orchestra. As a business, we only have two employees (myself being one of them). We don't spend money on advertising or publicity. But we do have around 200,000 followers on social media, including global music stars, former Australian prime ministers and, for a brief time, Mariah Carey.

The purpose of sharing these names and numbers is not *purely* to brag about creating a stonking big choir, but to dig further into the question: how on earth did this happen? Frankly, I'm as surprised as you are, particularly looking at my disappointing track record as a teacher. How did I convince so many people to buy a ticket to a show where they have to do the work by singing in public, when it is something that most of us are deeply uncomfortable doing?

The original social media post read:

> Calling all shower singers. Pub Choir is a choir for YOU. Bring your mates, bring your nan, just don't bring your kids coz it's in a pub. No sheet music, no auditions, no solos, no commitment, NO WORRIES! We'll teach you one song in three-part harmony in 90 minutes and then we'll never do it again. Come and let out some yells! $5 entry.

Seventy people came to the show. Seventy is already a lot of people for a choir! Fast forward one year to our first birthday show and 850 people lined up around the block for hours—in the rain—to get in.

What happens at Pub Choir? At the broadest level, it's kind of like a comedy show and a music lesson rolled into one. I divide the room into three sections and then in quick fire, teach the people in those three sections, different versions (harmonies) of the same song. By the end of the night when each section has learned their harmony, I combine them and the audience sings what they've learned. We video the moment where it comes together at the end of the night. I encourage people to put their phones away and to enjoy the sensation of working in literal harmony with strangers. When they get home, they can watch the video and relive their glory.

It's best to understand by hearing it. If you haven't had the chance but are interested, my personal favourite video is of Pub Choir performing 'Truly Madly Deeply' by Savage Garden from December 2019. There are around 3,000 people in the audience absolutely belting out one of Brisbane's most iconic songs, joined by Camerata, Queensland's Chamber Orchestra. In a cruel twist of fate, I lost my voice completely on stage during the show. It is quite an experience to be a vocal coach who is unable to speak, but have 3000 strangers share their voices with me instead.

This particular crowd felt so smug about their performance that they also raised $130,000 for Women's Legal Services that night. Pub Choir has donated over $300,000 to local community causes since 2018. People feel so good, so connected to their fellow singers at the show they empty their pockets, hoping that they can help somebody else feel as elated as they feel in that moment. What makes them feel *that* good?

I believe that Pub Choir gives people the opportunity to embrace and value mediocrity and truly, madly, deeply embrace their averageness. There is a freedom in a crowd where you are genuinely unimportant. Nobody believes that they have become a better singer at Pub Choir. They just feel less afraid to share whatever horrible voice they have. If one person forgets what to sing, someone nearby will remember. Some people sing flat, some sing sharp, some sing too early, some too late and the overall effect is a rich, full, electrifying average. Our audiences reclaim music-making back into their lives, realising that singing belonged to them all along.

Giving people the space to be average, even awful, and to still enjoy the singing experience, has been a revelation. We all deserve to feel joy, even if we're not 'the best'. This is an idea that the arts as a sector often struggles with. We love an eisteddfod, a competitive divide, a comparison between two often incomparable things. It seems particularly futile given there is no objective way to 'win' at music. We can measure ticket sales and social media followers, but there is no finish line to artistic pursuit.

Please don't mistake me: there is absolutely a place for kneeling at the altar of talent. But when we gather (pre-Covid-19) with 90,000 other fans to hear our musical idols at the stadium, yet take no steps to utilise our own creativity, we reinforce this unhelpful divide: Us, the millions of listeners on the one hand, and Them, our chosen musical elite on the other. We forget that we carry a free instrument inside our own bodies.

Now all this is well and good until a time comes when it's illegal to sing together. Thanks to Covid-19 this is the longest time in human history that we haven't sung together as a species—which has not been great for Pub Choir's business model. In March 2020, over the course of 24 hours, everything we had built disappeared overnight. I remember looking at my phone and seeing 20,000 Pub Choir tickets vanish in an afternoon. They still haven't come back. It was—and is—a terrible feeling.

With no work and a lot of time for introspection, I again asked myself what it was that I wanted to achieve. Pub Choir offered people a chance to sing badly with reckless abandon. It made them feel connected to each other. Was I now trapped by limitations of my own making, in which I could only imagine a 'choir' in one particular way? I went back to what I fundamentally knew: that our singing voices are with us wherever we go. And so Couch Choir was born.

Couch Choir runs on the same principles as Pub Choir: ordinary people sharing their voices as best they can. But rather than me teaching a live audience, I recorded myself singing the three harmonies. I posted the videos online for free, saying, 'Pick one video to learn, and when you're ready, film yourself singing along with me. Send that footage back to me, and I'll virtually edit you into a choir.' (I know we've all seen clips of virtual choirs and we're all a bit sick of it, but in March 2020, Couch Choir pioneered this activity worldwide.)

I thought maybe a hundred people would send in a video, because it's a lot to ask somebody to do: to send their singing voice to a stranger online and trust they won't betray you. Fifteen hundred people sent in a video in *three days* from all around the world. But even *more* incredible was that people were singing more gently, more thoughtfully than they ever did at Pub Choir. They were still terrible singers, but they had spent time with their own voice, accepted it, and sent it to me anyway.

Couch Choir showed me how transformative it could be to truly meet audiences where they were: in their own homes. The diversity within Couch Choir participants was remarkable. In one song we had 5,000 participants from 45 countries. We received submissions from places we had never considered visiting, like Kazakhstan and Norway. People sent videos from their farms, their wheelchairs, from houseboats, using sign language. They were younger, older, more colourful. Couch Choir was the distillation of what I had always hoped Pub Choir would be: regular, diverse people feeling personally empowered to contribute to the whole.

This newfound diversity didn't just give me a warm feeling but turned out to be good business sense. Our audience doubled in 2020, which, given the global context, was pretty incredible. The door to the corporate world opened. Businesses started writing to us from all around the world with events budgets they didn't know how to spend, and a work-from-home team that they didn't know how to connect.

Even more, I had the chance to pitch a TV show to SBS, which aired on 5 June, 2021. This was a wonderful opportunity to combine both the live Pub Choir show with the accessible, at-home Couch Choir. A world-first, two-hour, live-to-air experience, *Australia's Biggest Singalong*, saw 200,000 people tune in from home and learn to sing in harmony with one another (and Mark Seymour from Hunters & Collectors).

I'd love to conclude by saying that the upward momentum continues, but the truth is that I can see that my work is rapidly approaching a crossroads.

The current return of Pub Choir live shows feels tenuous at best. There is no certainty right now for artists, audiences or venues around Australia. I could advertise and sell tickets to a show that ends up being rescheduled six times before finally being cancelled. For two years, every attempt to stage a show has resulted in a financial loss. Pub Choir can't tour because we don't know which borders we can cross, and we certainly can't afford a snap two-week quarantine.

This uncertainty is compounded by the public demonisation of live music as an unsafe activity, despite the fact that the very same bodies breathe, cheer and sing at a football match. It's a disparity that existed long before Covid-19—arts vs. sport—but it is so stark now, at the time of writing, that 25,000 singing fans at a State of Origin is deemed safe, but no more than ten can dance at a wedding.

Furthermore, the shine on the novelty of an online experience has worn off. We're sick of our screens, and with each Couch Choir session the numbers dwindle.

Faced with the prospect of cancelling shows or singing to a non-existent online audience, artists are giving up, selling their equipment and getting other jobs. Musicians are flogging skincare and moisturisers on social media channels to make ends meet. I've been emceeing corporate events and singing at funerals. I don't know what the long-term consequences will be of decimating a whole cohort of creators, but we'll find out before too long.

What can be done?

I don't think we need more government grants. Not when they end up with established arts organisations anyway. Those gatekeeper companies will always survive. But I do wish that they'd bring an authoritative voice to the table and make the case to the decision-makers in this country, that the return of live music should be treated with the same urgency as the return of live sport.

As a small business owner, I wholeheartedly support the concept of vaccine passes that will allow vaccinated (and medically exempt) individuals to safely travel, work and congregate. Vaccinated audiences should be given the freedom to participate at Pub Choir with all the gusto of a crowd at a footy event. And if my support for an audience vaccine mandate is a shock to any Pub Choir follower, I would urge them to reflect upon the very concept of 'choir' itself. To join a choir is to agree to play a small part in a collective whole. You give of yourself, not for yourself, so that you may share in an outcome much bigger than yourself. Choir and herd immunity are conceptually intertwined.

We also need the private sector to see value in providing the arts as a valuable wellbeing experience for their workforce—i.e. as more than hiring a band for the Christmas party. Having corporate engagements has kept my business afloat when many of my peers have not been so lucky. Take your staff to the theatre. Book them a boozy art class on a Friday afternoon. If you're all still working from home, schedule an online, group singing lesson. And if it sounds too wishy-washy, go and read some peer-reviewed research on the benefits of group singing (spoiler alert: it's good for your health).

Perhaps most importantly I believe we need a new urgency in our own lives to create things ourselves, even poorly. For all the trauma around loss of purpose that Covid-19 has inflicted on artists everywhere, it has given us all an opportunity to reconsider everything that we do and why. To challenge every assumption we've ever held about how we create and connect.

I'll leave you with something positive to dwell upon. In September 2021, we completed another online Couch Choir project, with 613 participants from around the world. As they submitted their singing videos, we asked them four questions about how they felt. This is what they said:

Question	*Yes*	*No*	*Rather not say*
Did the experience of joining in with Couch Choir positively affect your mental health?	*100%*		
Did the experience of joining in with Couch Choir give you a sense of connection to others?	*98%*	*1%*	*1%*
Did the experience of joining in with Couch Choir give you a sense of hope for the future?	*96%*	*3%*	*1%*
Do you believe that the return of the performing arts should be a greater priority for State and Federal governments?	*96%*	*2%*	*2%*

Sure, it's not peer-reviewed research, it's just 613 people who chose to participate. But when 100 per cent of them self-report that their mental health is improved by joining in, it's worth taking note. Singing—even online—made them feel happier, more connected and more hopeful. And they thought it was an experience worth fighting for. Art has always been more than just entertainment or a distraction. Art can heal us.

Afterword:
Looking Back and Looking Forwards

Ian Maxwell
Cadigal and Darramuragal country

The challenges the performing arts face at the end of 2021 predate the current crisis. They are chronic, rather than acute. The pandemic has merely accelerated and exacerbated their existing trajectories. The sector trades on the enthusiasm of newcomers to the field, relying on a steady supply of youth, ambition, aspiration, enchantment, and, in more recent years, 'entrepreneurialism'. Our inclination is to applaud, and extol the virtues of such qualities, and we are all too frequently caught up ourselves in narratives of perseverance, resilience and resolute commitment to art. While these qualities are desirable and powerful, there is a brittleness to the outlook they engender: we associate success with moral fortitude, failure with weakness of resolve. Exhaustion, then, is integral to the field at the best of times. In the context of the acute crisis of the current Covid-19 epidemic, the arts eat their young.

The sector is exhausted. It is depleted and undernourished. Long before the extinction event of Covid-19, those who work in the performing arts in particular, and the arts sector in general, have endured injurious, precarious lives. Having functioned for decades with high levels of underemployment, industry-wide job insecurity, underpayment, the under-provision of workplace conditions and entitlements, industrial weakness and isolation, the arts are a case study for the future of work more generally—a canary in the coalmine of the 'gig' economy. We know, from recent research, if not personal experience, that the performing arts sector is the site of a perpetually unfolding mental health crisis that is pervasive, and, in a real sense, contagious. The systemic anxiety, stress, depression, and the corollaries of substance abuse, relationship breakdown and extreme dysfunction are not simply features of the cultural field, they constitute the fundamental architecture of modern Australian work as it is evolving.

On day two of the Authors' Convention, three speakers, David Pledger, Mark Williams and Julian Meyrick, were each invited to present a 20-minute talk—provocations, proposals or diagnoses—that addressed the over-arching theme of the Convention of imagination in economics and drew upon the back catalogue of the Platform Papers. They aimed to project a future in which that catalogue of work might provide, not just the basis for lobbying for the performing arts, but a peak advisory and policy-generating laboratory. Each speaker was asked to conclude their comments with three questions, which were put to the Convention for further discussion. Four key themes emerged. First, the proposition that art and culture are fundamental to the sustainability of society; second, that those engaged in the fields of art and culture do not have the capital to support them; third, that the arts are exhausted; and fourth, that its professionals have been pitted against each other in the competition for resources, with the result that the sector has become fragmented and unable to advocate for its interests as a whole. Let me tackle each of these in turn.

The fundamental nature of art and culture

Art and culture are not the 'icing on the cake' of the market economy, luxuries to be indulged when the budget allows. The economy should be in service of the culture it supports. Our culture is who we are: the thing that transforms us from aimless, isolated individuals into a society. It is a fundamental human drive, not just for 'self-expression' (a recent idea). It brings understanding to our existential and material circumstances, in play, invention, narrative and metaphor. Creative practices are universal constants across the diversity of human societies. Arguments can be made for their evolutionary value, but ultimately our stories are the means by which we share, refine, and maintain our discoveries, and how we integrate and sustain ourselves as a social organism. Art and culture are the binding agents that make the 'cake' of society possible.

What then is to be done? How can the arts claim a stake in the broader public sphere? What value, beyond Kantian abstraction on the one hand, and economistic utilitarianism on the other, do the arts in general, and the performing arts in particular, embody and assert? In the first presentation of the day, David Pledger offered a compelling case for 'interoperational synergies' with other sectors which he described as a form of 'social and cultural dramaturgy'. Taking a recent theatrical installation work, *Refuge* (2021), as an example, he described how the playful ways performing artists analyse social relationships have been used to explore the complex scenario of a simulated emergency response to a bushfire. Through such an approach, he argued, collaborative creative practice could extend beyond the aesthetic into other sectors. We have, David suggests, plenty to teach others about how to think about problems imaginatively, experimentally and experientially through creative practice.

The idea of 'interoperationality' is not to place the arts in service of yet another external social imperative, but to help identify what it is that the arts in general, and the performing arts in particular, *do*. They bring people into nuanced relationships on the basis of shared, collaborative undertakings. These relationships may be disruptive as readily as they are productive. Perhaps an argument could be made that the function of the arts in the economy is in fact 'disruption' (rather than, say, 'reflection', 'expression' or 'beauty'). In thinking through the other kinds of value propositions that we might make for the sector, the question of 'play' emerges. 'Play', not simply as opposed to *work,* or art understood as leisure (only marginally productive with a few wellbeing benefits attached) but 'play' as an inherently productive, creative, fundamental mode of being-in-the-world.

The missing capital

The arts lack capital, in the financial sense of reserves of cash and property, but more importantly in the abstract, philosophical sense of social power and political authority. We get left out of conversations. We don't have advocates in the room when important decisions are made that will affect our lives and industries. The sector has become fragmented in its responses, promoting individuals who trade on ideas of excellence: virtuosic skills passed on in professional settings. The hyper-focus on individual talent and professional qualifications has marginalised the sector, diminishing its capacity to advocate on its own behalf, or build up the practical know-how to do it well. One potential response to this is to integrate advocacy into arts courses, though some resistance might be anticipated from a number of quarters.

At this point, attention turned to the origins of this trend. Why has culture disappeared from the political agenda and disengaged from the public sphere at large? This is tangled territory, and a number of hypotheses were floated. All, however, spoke to the sidelining of the arts. We considered three dimensions of this retreat from engagement: first, a reduced view promulgated by the media of what the arts is; second, the eviscerating impact partisan politics has had on institutions which might otherwise unify the sector; and third, the contribution of cultural theory over the past fifty years to the politicisation of cultural practice, which ironically, it was observed, has helped to prevent cultural practice from gaining political purchase.

Some thought was given to the question of 'rights': the tension between socio-centric and ego-centric conceptions of the citizen and their responsibilities, and the competing virtues of collective versus individual action. As Justin O'Connor suggested, the idea of a collective 'right to culture' easily slips into an argument for the 'right of the artist' to express themselves (excellently), instead of recognising communal practices and committing to the provision of the arts as a fundamental social service. The left-leaning intelligentsia was given some responsibility in this regard, having allowed itself to slide away from its original commitment to civil and social rights into the fraught territory of identity politics, which readily lends itself to the logic of the free market and the rhetoric of autocracy. Has the legacy of the post-modern critique of culture mired the arts in a self-critical maze of reflexivity and, for want of a better word, relativism, that now prevents a direct, convincing story of their value?

Exhaustion

The exhaustion in the arts, and the theatre in particular, is not just a problem of scarcity of resources. The problem turns on the disjunction, if not the flat-out contradiction, between the practice of collaboration, on the one hand, and the logic of competition on the other. This tension fundamentally structures the field, regardless of the availability of actual resources. That is to say, even if more resources were available, the basic *agon* of the arts would not be disrupted. Actors, for example, enjoy the intense, collaborative, affirming and rewarding experience of joining a company for a period of rehearsal: a precious few weeks of camaraderie and shared labour, bonding and collaborative creativity. A week later, erstwhile collaborators find themselves in competition for the next role, the next opportunity to join a 'family'. How familiar is this experience! Recent research I conducted with Mark Seton and Marianna Szabo found abundant evidence of it, nowhere more emphatically than in the testimony of one actor, who wrote of the difficulty they had in determining which relationships with other actors were *real*. This contradiction lies at the heart of the actor's experience, from the competitive struggle to secure a place at acting school and build a sense of community during training, to the later efforts to secure an agent and vying for roles. It is a contradiction underpinned by a foundational discourse of virtuosity and exceptionalism which we use to frame the very concept of the *artist*: an individual whose value is determined by their distinction from the run of other professions and, indeed, humanity. Success in this contest is met with the rewards of celebrity, but these rewards do not supplant the right to a basic living wage.

Developing an argument for this right, Mark Williams described the hidden impact of financial insecurity on the lives of actors behind the glamorous curtain of celebrity, an impact exacerbated, but not caused by the pandemic lockdowns of 2020–21. Advocating for something like a universal basic income, he noted, 'the psychic satisfaction of working in the arts does not need to be matched with material riches: but as a matter of right matched to the basic needs of artistic citizens that are not currently served by contemporary economics: the tax breaks, the welfare and superannuation systems, and the like which other residents and taxpayers receive as a matter of course'. Exhaustion—of body, mind, and spirit—is the hardly surprising corollary of the current situation.

Competition for resources

While the logic of competition may arguably work (and a great deal hangs on 'arguably') to maximise the capacity of markets to generate and distribute the benefits of wealth, one of the fundamentals of performance is that without collaboration nothing happens. The 2021 Authors' Convention concluded with Julian Meyrick's careful archaeology of an attempt in 1946 to establish a broad-based, inclusive, democratically inspired national cultural agency in Australia, following the cascading disruptions of Federation, the Depression and world war. Perhaps the most important question to arise from it was simply what happened to that collective impulse? In historical terms, it appears to have been subsumed by the operational question of how to go about funding the arts. Perhaps the underlying question—what are the arts?—was too readily enlisted in the service of 'national identity'.

Ambiguity is the strength of art, as well as its weakness. Historically—indeed from Plato onwards—the protean, make-believe, *liminal* nature of theatre—and the recent genres that take up the even more equivocal trope of 'performance'—has generated profound anxiety and moral panics. One way forward is to embrace this fundamental ambiguity, perhaps in a systemic refusal to take a single position, a resistance to the increasingly strident demand that we always take sides, that we either 'like' or 'dislike', locked into a binary logic which brooks no middle ground, no 'both and', no considered uncertainty.

Julian's work on Australia's national theatre movement in the 1940s is not intended to point us (back) to a specific model but to remind us that our collective concerns are both perennial and contingent upon our *specific* current circumstances. Our challenge is to resist reprising old arguments that belong to the past, and instead peer through the lens of new experiences with the eye of imagination. That, I hope, is the project Currency House has set before us, and towards which the inaugural Convention of 2021 has made the critical first step.

Contributors

JONATHAN BIGGINS wrote *Satire—or Sedition: The threat to national insecurity* for Platform Papers in 2006. A versatile actor, director and writer, he has worked across theatre, opera, musicals and journalism, but is best known as a satirist. He is a member of the long-running annual *Wharf Revue* which he has co-directed for the Sydney Theatre Company since 2000. He is currently touring his one-man show *The Gospel According to Paul.*

RICHARD BRONK is an academic author, best known for *The Romantic Economist: Imagination in Economics* (2009). More recently, he was co-editor with Jens Beckert of *Uncertain Futures: Imaginaries, Narratives, and Calculation in the Economy* (2018). Richard graduated in Classics and Philosophy at Merton College, Oxford, before working for seventeen years in finance and the Bank of England. From there he joined the European Institute of the London School of Economics and Political Science, where he taught political economy from 2000–2007 and was a visiting senior fellow until July 2020. His work focuses on the role of imagination, language and metaphor in structuring economic behaviour and analysis, the epistemology of markets, and the history of ideas. https://www.imaginationineconomics.com

ASTRID JORGENSEN is the founding director of Pub Choir. She and her accompanist, Waveney Yasso, create spontaneous choirs in pubs. During the pandemic lockdown Pub Choir went online to become

Couch Choir, allowing would-be choristers to sing along from home, and it became a global phenomenon. Spinoff choirs, such as Scrubs Choir, played a vital role in supporting mental health as hospital doctors battled the pandemic. She draws upon her experience as a music educator, choral conductor, composer, and her love of pubs, to create musical experiences that are accessible and appealing to the whole community. In June, 2021, Pub Choir presented a live TV event, *Australia's Biggest Singalong* on SBS TV, with Julia Zamero, Miranda Tapsell and Mark Seymour. www.pubchoir.com.au

IAN MAXWELL is an Associate Professor and Head of the School of Literature, Art and Media in the Faculty of Arts and Social Sciences at Sydney University. The School has been a major support in planning the future of Currency House and the New Platform Papers, sponsoring the publication of the final issue in the first series, *On the Lessons of History* by Katharine Brisbane; a new e-edition of the entire series of Platform Papers, currently in production; and by hosting the inaugural convention of authors.

JULIAN MEYRICK is a Chief Investigator for Laboratory Adelaide, a research project studying the problem of value and evaluation processes in arts and culture. His book *Australian Theatre after the New Wave: Policy, Subsidy and the Alternative Artist* (2017) traces many of the problems Australian theatre is facing today back to the rise of the ethos of 'accountability' in the relationship between the artist and the State in the late 1970s. *In What Matters? Talking Value in Australian Culture* (2018), co-authored with Robert Phiddian and Tully Barnett, he looks at the legacy of this ethos in the language of contemporary policy making and argues that by changing the language, we may learn how to value culture better.

HARRIET PARSONS is an artist and independent researcher. She graduated from the Sydney College of the Arts in 1997 and exhibited regularly until 2011 in galleries in Sydney and Melbourne. She received a Master's degree from the Victorian College of the Arts in 2012 and completed her PhD on the collaborative drawing practices used by the artists on Captain James Cook's *Endeavour* at the School of Culture and Communication, Melbourne University, in 2019.

David Pledger is an artist, curator, writer, activist and producer who operates at the intersection of the performing, visual and media arts. He often performs in these roles simultaneously and retrospectively, in highly collaborative, constructed fields. The dramaturgical practice he has developed engages artists in all art forms, and experts across the social, scientific and academic spectrum, situating artistic practice in a broader cultural frame. He creates artworks and public events of scale that have multiple intentions and outcomes in the pursuit of progressive social change. He has written numerous articles, particularly on the relationship between art and climate change. https://www.davidpledger.com/about/

John Quiggin is a Professor in Economics at the University of Queensland and a prolific author. In the wake of the Global Financial Crisis, he made the prophetic warning in *Zombie Economics* that we must kill the dead ideas that still walk among us once and for all, or face 'an even bigger crisis in the future'.

Mark Williams is a practising lawyer to the arts, commercial and scientific community under his own name in Melbourne —and has been at the forefront of convergence issues including Federal and High Court cases on copyright infringement and the protection of confidential information. This includes work for software, telecommunications, film, television, computer games, music, stage and visual arts organisations. He holds postgraduate qualifications in intellectual property law (University of Melbourne, 1997) and a D.Phil. on seventeenth-century dramaturgy (University of Oxford, 1989). He wrote PP56 *Falling through the Gaps: Our Artists' Health and Welfare* in 2018. https://williamssolicitors.com/index.php/about-dr-mark-williams/

On the Lessons of History

KATHARINE BRISBANE

The final Paper in the original series, reprinted.

NO. 63

March 2021

Edited by
Julian Meyrick
and Harriet Parsons

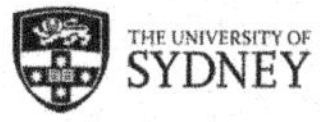

Acknowledgments

We acknowledge with gratitude our Partners in continuing support of Platform Papers and its mission to widen understanding of performing arts practice and encourage change when it is needed:

Neil Armfield, AO
Anita Luca Belgiorno-Nettis Foundation
Jane Bridge
Katharine Brisbane, AM
Elizabeth Butcher, AM
Penny Chapman
Dr Peter Cooke, AM
Sally Crawford
Wesley Enoch
Ferrier Hodgson
Larry Galbraith
Wayne Harrison, AM
Campbell Hudson
Lindy Hume
Professors Bruce King and Denise Bradley, AC
Justice François Kunc
Dr Richard Letts, AM
Peter Lowry, OAM and Carolyn Lowry, OAM
David Marr
Helen O'Neil
Lesley Power
Professor William Purcell
Queensland Performing Arts Centre Trust
Geoffrey Rush, AC
Dr Merilyn Sleigh
Maisy Stapleton
Augusta Supple
Christopher Tooher
Caroline Verge
Queensland Performing Arts Trust
Rachel Ward, AM and Bryan Brown, AM
Kim Williams, AM
Professor Di Yerbury, AM

To them and to all subscribers and Friends of Currency House we extend our grateful thanks.

Foreword

This is to be my last Platform Paper. Age and uncertain health brought about my decision in December 2019 to retire from the daily administration of Currency House. For some time we had been working on arrangements to secure the Papers' future under the aegis of a public institution, but from 2015 onwards, the political climate of arts funding and sponsorship had been steadily retreating. When the Covid-19 pandemic crept upon us in March 2020, we had already cancelled the Arts and Creativity breakfasts and we now suspended all our operations including the Papers. My daughter, Harriet Parsons, took advantage of the months of inactivity to restructure Currency House and find a permanent solution to our problems.

So in 2021 we are starting again. Julian Meyrick, a long-time friend and associate of Currency House, and now Professor of Creative Studies at Griffith University, has accepted the role of general editor of Platform Papers and Harriet has taken on the job of Director.

It only remains for me to thank full-heartedly all those who helped in wrangling together the myriad parts of this paper. Harriet was an essential part of achieving its finished form, in helping me to wrestle the detail of the material and clarify the moving timeline; and Julian Meyrick for using his understanding of our cultural history to support my argument. My thanks, equally, go to the other members of the Currency House Board and editorial committee for their support as we devised a way forward for Platform Papers at this time of cultural crisis. It's been a pleasure and a challenge to bring together the strength of all these creative voices and I hope they will be heard far and wide as we take this unique opportunity to together imagine Australia as a wiser and more creative country.

On the Lessons of History

It was the best of times. It was the worst of times. The millennium had just turned. Expectations of disaster had run high: about whether the mysterious new digital technology, on which we had so quickly come to depend, would bring the world to an end at midnight on 31 December? Its instrument was to be the algorithm in charge of the world's clocks, which had defined the date during the old century by two digits (99) and had to be revised to four (2000). Digital conversion, as we all came to understand, was not flexible, like the human brain. The change would transform the whole of world commerce, even as the rise of the digital age laid out a new world before us. Were we to call this first decade of the twenty-first century the noughties?

This paper ruminates on the concerns that have occupied the arts sector in Australia during this century so far: the decisions we have made, the disasters we have survived and the opportunities that are now open to make us a kinder, more congenial society. The reader will have deduced, if they are not old enough to remember, that the end of the world did not occur at midnight on 31 December 1999. How many of our other expectations have changed since then?

Who could have imagined twenty years ago that a virus, uncovered in a wet market in China, would spread right round the world in 2020, and reach epic proportions in the space of three or four months? The pandemic continues at the time of writing but the forced hiatus has given us time at Currency House to refresh our thinking, reflect on the work of the past two decades and restructure.

To this end I have gathered up the 62 Platform Papers and begun an overview of their contribution to the events that have impacted upon the arts since the Millennium. Not every paper has made it into the finished text but each has brought fresh insight into the reasons why the nation's creative instinct has, in our view, been systematically suppressed. And the full list is printed with the Endnotes.

In great part the picture in the arts has been of a young country, of colonial origins, that for most of its history has refused to recognise the creative management of the land practised by our First Nations people and blindly deferred to the customary practices of its great and powerful friends. And who today amid extraordinary global change is timidly attempting to transform our old structure as a middle-sized nation trading primary goods into an intellectual, multicultural global thinker.

The exploration has left me with one question in particular. Why, at the start, when the Government set up a system in support of the creative arts in 1968, was the Australia Council's funding directed at the product rather than the creator? In the first year of the life of the Australia Council, those of us who were there, with a head full of ideas but too little experience, grasped at a huge opportunity to shape the future of the arts. Jean Battersby, as founding director of the Council, proposed that for funding and management purposes we should divide up the arts sector by genre or 'artform', a shoddy word that has regulated Council planning ever since. Art is a quality that can be applied to a myriad of forms but has no form of its own. It is an expression of certain values. This decision made the 'form' the focus of the Boards that were duly set up, rather than the artists and their needs. As artists experimented, the 'artforms' proliferated; and projects were regularly rejected because they 'fell outside the guidelines'. As a result, over time, the output has been allowed to overshadow the benefit to society of artists themselves.

As Dorothy Hewett once said to me, art is the detritus of the creative process. Valuing the product over the creator places the Australia Council in the same category as Centrelink. It asks our artists to 'work for hours': that is, to allocate their time in a way that will enable a profitable outcome. Some creative people have devised such a way to make a living. Some have even prospered. But how many of these fortunate creators count the value of their practice in terms of hourly cost? My guess is that they would say they work at their chosen practice because they cannot do otherwise. It is their vocation.

When we arrived at the turn of the century, the last decade had been a nervous one. Paul Keating's Labor Government had given us a rush of radical reforms: the Native Title Act, compulsory superannuation, enterprise bargaining, privatisation of QANTAS and the Commonwealth Bank, the creation of APEC and a Republic Advisory Committee. There had been much to digest. So in 1996, for those who voted him in, John Howard's promise of 'relaxed and comfortable' government came as a welcome relief. The Coalition won a massive 45-seat majority and Australia settled down to the prospect of a reliable, if rather boring, decade.

However, within weeks we were shaken from this dream by what came to be known as the Port Arthur Massacre. Martin Bryant's rampage on 28 April 1996, left 35 dead, many more wounded and holds the record for the worst mass murder in modern Australian history. Howard's swift action on gun control caught voters by surprise; but the moral authority he won by his handling of that event was squandered in 2001, on the eve of his third term as prime minister, by the stand he took against the Norwegian vessel MV *Tampa.* Its Captain, Arne Rinnan, had rescued 433 mainly Afghan refugees from a fishing vessel in international waters off our north-west coast. When he attempted to land them on Christmas Island SAS troops were ordered to board the ship.

Howard's hard line on the refugees was vindicated in the eyes of the popular press when, a month later, on 11 September 2001, two hijacked American Airlines planes, and their helpless passengers, smashed into Manhattan's World Trade Center, killing 3,000 men and women as they descended on New York's financial heart at the beginning of a working day. We knew that our safe, parochial, middle power, so far from the fears of the world's trouble spots, would never be the same.

I had dined at the Windows on the World restaurant in the North Tower of the World Trade Centre only months before the attack. My companion and I stood looking down at the ant-like figures scurrying along the street below, like Harry Lime on the Ferris wheel in *The Third Man*. 'No wonder the Americans think they are masters of the world,' I said. But the world no longer thinks so today.

Where was I when I heard the news of this world-changing massacre? I had sold our family home and awoke that morning in my friend Jean Cooney's apartment to the sound of the radio urging us to turn on the television. We watched, hypnotised, as first one and then the other twin tower crumbled almost silently. It happened so slowly we could see the victims as they fell from the windows. That day I closed the door on 87 Jersey Road, Woollahra, which had been my home for 35 years, and the place where Philip and I had established Currency Press, with Jean as my colleague and assistant. Currency and I were now awaiting the completion of the Press's new offices in Cleveland Street, Redfern, to which we were adding a rooftop apartment for me. Closing one more door meant opening another.

In October, the Government claimed that refugees from another vessel were now threatening to throw their children overboard. The claim was proved false; but in November, another election secured another substantial majority for the Coalition. Howard summarily introduced and passed his Border Protection Bill and the *Tampa's* Afghan refugees were deported to Nauru. Over Christmas, in a mixture of excitement and weariness, the Currency staff and I moved into our new home.

In October 2002 Australians experienced the horrors of terrorism firsthand. The Bali bombing of a popular tourist site killed 88 Australians, 38 Indonesians and 28 Britons; and their personal stories were published beside those of asylum seekers in the media. The rising tide of refugees escalated public concern for their safety as they risked their lives on the way to Australia. At the same time, it also heightened Islamophobia. Our refugee policy, once seen as contributing to economic growth, was transforming our reputation by leaps and shocks, from a welcoming nation, made up of generations of immigrants, into one that builds detention centres and imposes regulations to ensure that 'we decide who comes to our country and the manner in which they come'.

As opinion polarised we began to lose our trust in the society we thought we understood. *What kind of Australia are we becoming?* we wondered.

John Howard continued in office until 2007 when Labor under Kevin Rudd won a crushing victory ('Kevin '07') in which Howard himself lost his seat of Bennelong to Walkley award-winning journalist Maxine McKew. Rudd's elevation excited public expectations: here was a new breed of parliamentarian, one fluent in Chinese, who would lead reform and strengthen our ties with Asia and the Pacific. Peter Garrett, lawyer and rock star, became a high profile Minister in a number of portfolios. His role as Arts Minister raised particular hopes; a familiar face and someone who knew what living as a performer was like, but the pace of reform came too fast. 'Mistakes were made', as they say; Rudd alienated his allies and it all fell apart in a coup.

Labor did not reverse the policy on refugees.

Two distinct forces have shaped the changes since 2000. The first is the digital world, which encouraged autonomy and social fragmentation; the second, the voice of growing Aboriginal authority. At the start, the internet, which allowed anyone to publish an opinion online, was seen as a triumph of democracy; but mass online publishing diminished the profits of the print publishers by delivering their content free, and undermined their authority by discarding the supervision of editors.

It has also given rise to 'trolling', the fatal flaw in social media. Traditional publishers have policies about what they will and will not publish; the social media have armies of 'moderators' instead, who take offensive information down, but only after it has been published and the damage is already done. Editors protect civil society. Their loss has been especially bad for newspapers. Today, newspapers who once delivered authoritative journalism compete with the digital media to deliver intimate, heart-breaking stories via multiple portals in vibrant colour and with breathless speed. Since September 11, the media's capacity to bring death and disaster, triumph and glory, to our living rooms, has never been so great.

But as the authority of the press has fragmented, one voice has grown in strength and unity: that of our Indigenous leaders, including in the performing arts. Steady progress was made towards reconciliation in the 1980s and 1990s, including the establishment of a Council for Aboriginal Reconciliation, the Mabo decision, which rejected the historical fiction of *terra nullius*; and on 28 May 2000, over five hours, 250,000 people walked across the Sydney Harbour Bridge in the cause of reconciliation. There were similar events in Brisbane and Melbourne.

But in 2007 this goodwill was dealt a blow when allegations of widespread sexual abuse of Aboriginal children were made by the Victorian State Crown Prosecutor, Nanette Rogers, SC. This led Howard to order the Northern Territory National Emergency Response. Little was achieved. The unexpected deployment of Army troops against Australian citizens only revived traumatic memories for the Stolen Generations of the forcible removal of children from their parents. A decade later, it was the energetic management of those Aboriginal elders who signed the Uluru Statement from the Heart that finally began to break down the walls of mutual fear and anger that had for so long been a major hindrance to healthy debate.

The Uluru Statement is a simple, moving document, composed for the 2017 First Nations National Constitutional Convention on the lands of the Anangu people and accepted by consensus of all 250 delegates. It has become a familiar point of reference, a guide to quiet conversation between multicultural Australia and its first nations.

Publications by Indigenous authors, like Bruce Pascoe's *Dark Emu* (2014), broke through the racial divide of unthinking oppression in other ways, by bringing their research into the body of knowledge about cultural and agricultural science, astronomy, fire, drought and flood management, family and social harmony, and moral regulation. Given the evidence of historical injustice, the squabbling in Parliament and lack of even basic courtesy shown by our then Prime Minister Malcolm Turnbull's swift rejection of the Statement from the Heart, it is astonishing that our indigenous elders have still found a means to prevail with their soft voices. The Uluru Statement will not go away.

For Australia this has been a period of cultural change from which we have emerged a different nation. So far we have learnt much about how power works but nothing about how to wield it on the global stage. We only know that the giant act of vandalism called September 11 surpassed anything we had known before. In the years since 2001, we have allowed ourselves to become swept up in our fears and occupied with distractions—new devices of incomprehensible ingenuity that invite entry into dazzling new worlds to escape the wreck we have made of this one. It has taken until 2020 for a new kind of change—drought, floods, earthquakes, famine and now global plague—for our stubborn hearts to make the turn towards a more rational way of life and public and community trust.

The Genesis of the Papers

In the 1970s, arts support expanded under the aegis of the Australia Council, and by the 1980s artists and arts organisations were largely dependent on regular government grants, but when funding began to contract in the 1990s, this dependence made practitioners fearful of speaking out. By the turn of the twenty-first century global upheaval and political polarisation were also increasing the mood of despondency among arts workers. Something was needed to restore, from the fragments of our culture, the arts' mirror on the world. We needed a national conversation about the breadth of artistic endeavour and why we define it as part of the common good. So in 2001 my colleagues and I began a monthly discussion club in Sydney and called it Currency House. We became a not-for-profit affiliate of Currency Press, which also gave us a home.

But the silence that had possessed so many working artists meant that persuading people to talk about their problems was not easy. Self-esteem was low, confessing weakness inadmissible: however desperate things got, it was a professional necessity for artists to appear always 'in demand', a hollow defence of the itinerant worker to prevent temporary unemployment becoming permanent.

We solved the problem by introducing the Chatham House rule to our monthly debates. The public issues thus raised in private became the inspiration, in 2004, for a quarterly essay dedicated to the working life of those in the creative sector (as it has come to be called) and the support systems on which they depend. We settled on four issues a year supported by a committee under the general editorship of the plan's initiator, Dr John Golder from the School of Theatre Studies at the University of NSW.

Reading the earliest papers again in 2020, in which we set out to document the causes of the malaise, I am astounded by the authors' percipience. They exude a pent-up energy and courage in their targeting of social causes and proposals for betterment. But even more surprising is the accuracy of the forecasts. Disappointingly, for those who shared those early days with me, few of their innovations (or good intentions) have yet been vested in public policy. To those in the know, this is no surprise.

In the last twelve months we have experienced fire and flood, the greatest modern Australia has seen, followed by the Covid-19 pandemic, which within four months silently swept around the world, dividing families, causing myriad deaths, closing business and entertainment, and locking down state borders and communities. Governments are now working overtime to find ways to save the economy.

The continuing months of isolation have brought a change in priorities and even a change of heart about the purpose of the public money that furnishes federal and state incomes, and the importance of social policy over productive employment, in times of depression or disaster. The succession of shocks that landed on an unprepared nation, has forced the disturbing realisation on Australians that we are no longer protected by distance from our global responsibilities, nor excluded from its dangers. With remarkable stoicism the Coalition's leaders have released billions of dollars, not just to those seeking a job, but for those seeking a life.

But now that it looks as though another year may pass before we see the back of this pandemic, panicky voices are beginning to rise, fearful of the changes this global pause for thought will bring about. As in the early days of the Platform Papers, now is the time for a proper national conversation: to listen, to speak out, and to be heard.

Coordinating the Voices

The Platform Papers series quickly became a record of the mood of the times. The aim was not to write a history series but to add to our understanding of the present and ways to bring about a better future. The brief to authors became a four-point structure comprising an account of

1. the state of the subject under scrutiny;
2. its history and social causes;
3. new directions that might be taken; and finally,
4. a challenge to the reader with a new idea or provocation to move forward.

This has proved a sound framework on which to hang 60-plus issues over 16 years. The authors' chosen themes have ranged from industry work practices to environmental sustainability, public policy, export, finance, censorship, copyright, welfare and all genres of the performing arts including film, television and an increasing variety of digital media.

The need for change has been expressed palpably in each paper. Each has met a challenge, sometimes receiving criticism, at other times gratitude for enabling an important argument to be heard. The question of what it means to be an Australian, and where this leads us, haunts them all.

What follows will give a brief insight into the principal issues that have preoccupied our authors. We asked them to raise new, provocative questions about the purpose of the arts and the conditions under which artists work. The first authors we approached responded with a cautious promise to think it over, but once they began, the writing came like a long exhale of breath, leaving them exhausted and exhilarated, although still fearful of standing up to defend their precarious way of life.

The Rise of the Digital Realm

At the outset the rise and rise of the digital realm was hailed as the discovery of a new democratic playing field for the creative mind. The technological change came with frightening speed and power. The years 2004 to 2006 saw the launch of the social media platforms Facebook, YouTube and Twitter. Digital expansion allowed anyone to publish an opinion, instantly world-wide, in exchange for no more than their personal data—name, city, date of birth, and what they 'like'. The flood of 'free' information undermined the profits of the commercial media and put news organisations in particular under pressure. It also detached publishing in the public domain from the 'gatekeepers' of copyright protection, journalistic integrity and censorship.

By 2010 we had come to realise the ruthlessness of the game we were in, the all-consuming nature of the new technology, and it changed the face of arts publishing forever. Shilo McClean was exhilarated by the vision of the new democratic creative freedom the digital realm offered—the chance for all of us to be creative—but warned of the way the corporate world was engaging with innovation in PP no.24, *The Digital Playing Fields: New rulz for film art and performance*. New stores of data stretched beyond imagination, but the pressing challenge now was how to ensure that the daily news was reliable:

> It is an established pattern that innovation is followed by commercial exploitation, which eventually trends to a situation of monopoly or duopoly in the control of production. The pattern is so common one might even think it inevitable. Indeed, it could be argued that the ensuing stagnation that arises once a field is dominated by powerbrokers is in fact a condition that is a prerequisite for further innovation. [PP24, pp.5–6]

By 2020 uncertainty had become a way of life. Having learned to live with flexible employment and flexible income, we now have to negotiate 'fake news'. In 2004 the author of PP no.1, Martin Harrison, was already sounding the alarm. He was the founding producer of the ABC's Radio Arts (now defunct) and presenter of Books and Writing. In *'Our ABC' a Dying Culture? One way forward in arts programming*, he warned:

> The ABC is not fulfilling its Charter obligations in relation to the arts. There is a long history of budget cuts, poor management appointments, poor policy decisions, Federal Government interference and a lack-lustre Board, which lie, in large measure, behind the declining significance of the ABC. [PP1, p.1]

The Australian Broadcasting Corporation, founded in the 1930s as the Australian Broadcasting Commission, was modelled on the BBC with its Charter of objectives. As the independent dispenser of free public information, the ABC's charter was intended to protect it from external pressures, but an ever-shrinking budget, coupled with performance measures based on commercial standards, meant that it was struggling to serve the public good. Inexplicably, profit had somehow taken over from ethics as the measure of good governance. The metaphor, so deplored by economists, that governments, like households, must live within their means, had reframed the arts as entertainment—an indulgence that should be foregone in difficult times—rather than an indispensable asset of a thinking society.

Harrison's modest suggestions for enlarging the arts coverage were politely received and ignored and ABCTV programming began to include an increasingly large proportion of safe British 'bonnet' dramas. Today, in the commercial sector, the channels survive, but with only a shadow of their former ratings.

In 2009 Ian David, veteran screenwriter and director of many award-winning series, gave an insider's view of the television industry in his PP no.21, *Television: What will rate in the new tomorrow?* On-line streaming had forced the free-to-air services to seek out new ways of attracting audiences and he deplored the flood of 'reality TV' shows and general decline in the quality of content—but he concluded that, despite the assault on its ratings, television was here to stay.

Kim Dalton, a former Head of ABC Television, again tackled the issue of the ABC's integrity in 2017, reporting bitterly that there had been no favourable advance since he left in 2013. In PP no.51, *Missing in Action: The ABC and Australia's screen culture*, he too deplored the reduction in local production and argued that the ABC Charter was outdated, with no provision for transparency or accountability.

> The only guidance in regard to Australia's cultural output and its creative community is the requirement that it should 'encourage and promote the musical, dramatic and other performing arts in Australia'. Arguably a very narrow, somewhat old-fashioned, and potentially elitist, instruction that ignores whole areas of contemporary creative practice including screen production. Beyond the Charter, though, there is no indication from government of just what the ABC is meant to do, how it is meant to do it and to what end. [PP51, p.35]

In 2020, however, the Covid-19 pandemic has given the ABC an opportunity to regain its strength as a unifying social force as Australians struggle to engage with a new normality. Rural and remote communities, tourists and city dwellers, have relied on its local radio emergency services and coverage of the bushfires, some for their lives. It is a great shame that, when its programming on radio and TV has responded so well to its role as a regional communicator, the economic crisis has prompted further budget cuts, further loss of valued staff from studios in Australia and around the world, and further loss of services. Since 2014 the ABC has lost $100 million a year in budget allocations. Some of the most respected and longest serving public broadcasters and their programs have gone from our airwaves.

The government sector and those who, like the arts, depend on its funding, have suffered with the ABC the effects of economic policies that prioritise private sector growth over expenditure on the public good.

As traditional radio, television and film lost territory to social media, terrorists were among the earliest adopters of the new technology. They used it to recruit members and inform the world of their atrocities. In 2006 the federal Government announced its intention to reinvigorate the old sedition laws but, as so often in the past, the first casualty was not treason but satire, civil society's protection against government over-reach. In PP no.10, *Satire—or Sedition? The threat to national insecurity* Jonathan Biggins, actor, comedian, writer and creative member of the annual Wharf Revue, mounted a defence of free speech.

> Within days of the Bill's introduction, a broad coalition of artists, performers, journalists, publishers and civil libertarians condemned the proposed laws as a threat to free speech. Why, they asked, were the existing sedition laws, last used in this country in the early 1960s, and effectively defunct ever since, being revitalised at this time when practically every other Western democracy had removed the crime of sedition from their statutes? [PP51, p.52]

Biggins' Paper gives a history of the Sydney Theatre Company's annual Wharf Revue since its launch in 2000 and includes a Faustian dialogue in mock-Elizabethan verse, in which a fictional Philip Ruddock, an apparently dutiful but minor cabinet minister, makes a pact with the Devil (Nick Minchin, then Minister for Finance and Administration) for a term in the portfolio of Attorney General. When Minchin comes for his soul, Ruddock escapes damnation by claiming that the contract he signed in blood is 'open to interpretation' and his soul was only leased.

So wily Ruddock to his word was true
And stood with Reith as truth went overboard.
In Tampa's wake he steered his Party through,
His place beside his matter now assured.
The borders shut, as iron walls descended
Against poor souls left stateless and adrift.
Unburdened by his soul he now ascended,
Unshaken by a public family rift.
The eyes that once on tenderness reflected,
Now blankly lizard-like unblinking stared.
Incompetence concealed went undetected
While lawyer's tongue lashed anyone who cared. [PP10, p.48]

National laws of sedition and censorship limited law-abiding printers and publishers, but did little to rein in anonymous destructive assaults launched from the international no man's land of the internet; and the regulatory confusion had other systemic effects.

In PP no.12, *Film in the Age of Digital Distribution* (2007) Richard Harris bravely navigated a course through the problems it was causing for film distributors. The introduction of multiple platforms added new layers of complexity for the distribution of films to exhibition houses. While recognising the opportunities they offered, Harris, who subsequently became executive director of the Australian Screen Directors' Association, warned that the industry should not lose sight of the value of its traditional broadcasting rights:

As we look to the options, it is important to keep in mind that while this new media landscape is opening up the conventional media world

> will continue to dominate. Furthermore, these broadcasters will still require access to spectrum, which will remain a valuable public resource. In other words, while strategies for future media need to be developed, broadcasting regulations will remain as relevant as ever and need to be modified and augmented. [PP12, p.58]

By 2013 the familiar paths to success, particularly for the local film industry had broken down, and, according to Lauren Carroll Harris in PP no.37, *Not at a Cinema Near You: Australia's film distribution problem*, distribution had succumbed to the effects Richard Harris had foreseen.

Economics, Cultural Policy and Government Funding

The internet transformed our culture, but it was a change in taxation law in 2000 that had the most profound effect on the arts. The introduction of the Australian Business Number (ABN) turned artists into 'small business owners'. No longer objects of patronage, they were free to trade in their own name, and their daily practices became the business activities of budding entrepreneurs.

In the years that followed, artists developed interdisciplinary practices that merged the interpretive and authorial roles of actors, directors and writers in collaboration. However, as time went on, the adoption of corporate measures such as the key performance indicator (KPI) made funding agencies increasingly more of a hindrance than a help. Funding the arts requires a set of criteria, but the combination of old funding categories based on genre and company size, mixed with business measures, such as audience 'reach', placed obstacles in the way of innovation.

At the start of our Papers, in 2004, Christopher Latham, violinist and music festival director, wrote in PP no.2, *Survival of the Fittest: The artist versus the corporate world*, that making art had become an act of market competition:

> The last thirty years have seen management displace the creators to become the powerful figures of the arts world. [...] Increasingly, even the section of artistic talent has been seen slipping from the hands of the sector towards the marketing and sponsorship departments [...] Australia needs its artists to initiate change, to rethink the present in the light of the past and begin to invest in a body of work that will in turn become their legacy. [PP2, p.12 passim]

The use of business language was also causing a kind of social amnesia in the arts. It was making us forget the history of how we had come to do what we do and what we value among our achievements. Julian Meyrick, director and academic, described a theatre sector that was unable to incorporate the legacy of the past into its work in the present because it was at odds with its history.

In PP no.3, *Trapped by the Past: Why our theatre is facing paralysis*, he argued that the 'modern repertoire had been adapted to accommodate the philanthropy of the corporate world. Although some plays from the past were being revived with respectful performances, the productions displayed little knowledge of the conventions of the author's time or background'.

> I have briefly described how this tradition played out in the unique soil of Australia; how it was transformed in the 1970s into a wholly distinctive mode of dramatic production; how inter-generational

> understanding between different practitioners was lost; and how we are today headed for exactly the same kind of impasse. What I have been working towards is the idea of wholeness—that artists working in Australian theatre are connected by myriad invisible wires, and each of these sings with specific, but nevertheless, shared, experience. [PP3, p.52]

In PP no.4, *The Myth of the Mainstream: Politics and the performing arts in Australia today* (2005), cultural activist Robyn Archer proposed that modern marketing had sold the idea to the Australian public that its culture was homogenous. Whether the subject was race, sex or music, the 'mainstream' had its opinion. As a result, public commentary was losing its critical edge. It was important, she argued, for the press to distinguish between entertainment and intellectual challenge.

In 2005 it was hard to find an author brave enough to write about the Australia Council, which was becoming the subject of dissension. Confidence was at a low ebb and artists were reluctant to bite the hand that fed them. Keith Gallasch took up the challenge with PP no.6, *Art in a Cold Climate: Rethinking the Australia Council.* As the founding co-editor, with Virginia Baxter, of the journal *RealTime,* he had fought to retain informed critical writing on the arts. Gallasch's mood reflected the rage and gloom felt in the sector over the decline in public respect for the arts. In December 2000, without warning or consultation the Australia Council had announced a restructure that would include shutting down the New Media Arts Board. What conditions, what public attitudes, had compelled this decision? he asked:

> Like the universities, like industry—and like them, through research and innovation—the arts have a responsibility to a future Australia. Have we become complacent at all levels about our capacity to invent? [PP4, p.38]

The authors of Platform Papers so far had shown that artists could explain what was going wrong in their own particular sectors, but they found it much harder to mount a general defence of the arts. It was becoming increasingly apparent that the diverse values they were defending carried little weight separately and required a cultural policy to protect them. To date we still have only one such document, Creative Nation, initiated by Prime Minister Paul Keating in 1994.

In 2006 David Throsby, with PP no.7, *Does Australia Need a Cultural Policy?* outlined an approach to legislation that would provide criteria for measuring social and economic value. He pointed to the way our culture is embedded in the country's social and economic policies, and advised that our cultural values should be recognised in legislation at every level of government. Legislation is either top down or bottom up, he wrote, and in the case of culture he opted for bottom up.

> A cultural policy is not a single document or statement or piece of legislation. It is the collection of actions that the government takes to create the conditions under which our cultural values, and indeed our whole cultural life, can find their expression. I have suggested that at the present moment in Australia's development we need a re-evaluation of what constitutes our cultural policy in this broad, all-embracing sense. I have drawn attention to some of the conflicting messages that bring about the need. [PP7, p.46]

He also asked why Australia had abstained from voting on a UNESCO draft Universal Declaration on Cultural Diversity, which in 2005 had

> focused worldwide attention on the importance of culture as an expression of fundamental human values [...] and elevated the role that cultural policy can, and should, play in national and international policy. Of the 154 delegates, 148 had voted in favour. The US and Israel voted against.
>
> [...] Why did we take such a conspicuously oppositional stand in an international arena where the diplomatic implications of voting behaviour do not go unnoticed? It is tempting to read Australia's abstention as simply another gesture of support for our great and powerful ally, and indeed this is exactly how it was interpreted. The official explanation, however, is based on technicalities, including concern that some aspects of the convention might conflict with our domestic policies. [PP7, pp.30–31]

Throsby listed the conflicting messages coming from the Howard Cabinet at that time and suggested that we should begin by defining what we meant by culture and believed our culture to be.

Since publication, the arguments have continued. Throsby's Paper makes a valuable guide for anyone strong enough to take up the challenge of defining our cultural policy. In 2018, we asked if the climate was yet right for a new attempt. He returned to the question, and in the course of writing PP no.55, *Art, Politics, Money: Revising Australia's cultural policy*, reluctantly came to the conclusion that the answer was 'no'.

***

Choreographer Amanda Card was the first of our authors to point to the gaps in the Australia Council's project funding regulations, with PP no.8: *Body for Hire? The state of dance in Australia* (2006). Traditionally, dance had been hierarchical: choreographers dictated the movements and dancers were 'bodies for hire'. Now, in 2006, more collaborative forms of dance were emerging and Australia was at the forefront, but the Australia Council's 'Organisation Program' was not making life any more secure for small companies:

> A case in point is De Quincey Co. Over the past six years the Sydney-based organisation, headed by Tess De Quincy, has 'enjoyed' an erratic and potentially fatal engagement with the Australia Council category. The company was granted Key Organisation Program funding in 2002, but not 2003. They were back on the list in 2004, but off again in 2005. This funding category should offer small organisations relief from the continuous merry-go-round of applications and recipients assume (rightly so) that it gives vital support to develop a small infrastructure to sustain the company. [PP8, p.17]

In a mixture of excitement, over the renewal that had been achieved in modern dance by Australia Council funding in the 1980s, and exasperation at the lack of understanding that she saw as having undermined its progress since, Card called for a new system: a new way of employing choreographers and a better deal for dancers to re-invigorate dance once again.

Five years later Erin Brannigan, in PP no.25, *Moving Across Disciplines: Dance in the twenty-first century,* recorded the breakup of the old hierarchical relationship between the choreographer and the dancer; and in 2019 Sue Healey in PP No.60, *Capturing the Vanishing: A choreographer and film,* described a new way of escape—by embracing film. Dancefilm had opened a new career for her as a combined choreographer and photographer which has given her the independence to develop her work and enabled her dancers to be seen around the globe.

***

Despite some wins and a sustained period of economic growth, the arts were still not flourishing. In the search for an answer, the idea of building 'creative industries' was raised. In PP no.9, *What Price a Creative Economy?* (2006), Stuart Cunningham made a case for adopting the language of business and economics to frame the humanities, as a way of valuing the creative sector. However, if anything, this exercise served only to demonstrate how difficult—and disheartening—it was to harness culture's 'intrinsic' value to commercial gain. Artists were brought in on business and scholarly ventures, to add their insights to research, but while their skills provided éclat and style, the promised key to innovation eluded them. The concept struggled on for a decade and died of natural causes.

Lyndon Terracini, meanwhile, was turning the focus on the artist in the community. He had made his operatic career as a baritone in Europe before settling in Lismore in 1988. As the founding director of the Northern Rivers Performing Arts (NORPA), he had championed the commissioning and production of new operatic works in regional New South Wales; and, as director of the Queensland Music Festival 2000–05, mounted and locally produced popular music, dance and comedy shows with community performers, in small towns around the state. In PP no.11, *A Regional State of Mind: Making art outside metropolitan Australia* (2007), he argued for the need to make and create art in our own backyard:

> ... a reassessment of our perceived view of the relationship between amateur and professional organisations is needed. We need to look at the rough origins of our theatre and where we have taken it in the last thirty years. Then we might begin to see with new insight and different criteria, the store of energy contained in life outside our capitals. We might begin to acquire a regional state of mind. [PP11, p.33]

Sadly, when he was appointed artistic director of Opera Australia two years later, his 'music of place' was not an element of his new administration.

The division between big and small had become irreconcilable and artists were searching for financial arguments for their defence. Academics Kay Ferres and David Adair quantified the contribution of the arts to the national economy. In PP no.14, *Who Profits from the Arts*? (2007) the authors traced the intricate social and financial connections between our cities' entertainment quarters and the theatres within them, for a project funded by the Australia Council. In PP no.15, *A Sustainable Arts Sector? What will it take?* (2008), Cathy Hunt and Phyllida Shaw, two arts strategists, followed with a collaborative plan for arts subsidy involving the public and private sectors. Hunt, with her company Positive Solutions, has since enabled extensive government support for community arts activity in regional Queensland.

Also in 2008 jazz guru Peter Rechnievski analysed the problems in the jazz scene, which, for all its apparent economic success, was delivering to musicians only the barest of livings. His

PP no.16, *The Permanent Underground: Australian contemporary jazz in the new millennium* supported a boost to the creation of a national collective of jazz artists and audience.

National identity has always been a part of the Australia Council's remit. In PP no.17, *What is an Australian Play? Have we failed our ethnic writers?* (2008), Chris Mead asked how this intent should be defined by the funding regulators:

> Australia has a turbulent present with a fragmented, hybrid population that continually renegotiates theorists' attempts to analyse them via class or post-colonialism. Xenophobia, distance, charity, religious freedom, migration, a rich land and a diverse people—all these combine to make Australia an extraordinary culture. But how much of that turbulence or difference reaches our stages? [PP17, p.6]

At the end of 2008, with PP no.18, *Getting Heard: Achieving an effective arts advocacy*, former Shadow Arts Minister, Chris Puplick, closed the debate, advising artists that they must build unity of purpose within the sector before they could effectively lobby government for support. Groups who achieved an appointment with the Minister would find that time and attention was limited and applicants must be ready to speak briefly, cogently and with one voice—and leave a summary behind. Today this advice remains good.

***

In 2007 had seen the end of the Howard Government years in a landslide victory for the ALP under Kevin Rudd. Rudd began his term in office by convening the '2020 Summit' of experts, to construct a long-term, bi-partisan, strategy for the nation's future. The year 2008 found us in a fever of reform: Australia signed the Kyoto Protocol on climate change, drew up an emissions trading scheme, delivered a National Apology to the Stolen Generation, and introduced stimuli like the Education Revolution, funding new buildings; and a home insulation scheme, which faltered after a series of accidents, but all this was overshadowed by the global financial crisis. Rudd went out on a limb, spent $500billion on stimulus; and Australia survived without a recession. Despite these early successes, internal pressures split the party in 2010, resulting in a 'coup' in which Julia Gillard became Australia's first female prime minister.

In 2009 we turned attention again to the big picture and published PP no.19, *'Your Genre is Black': Indigenous performing arts policy.* Hilary Glow and Katya Johanson, with 18 Indigenous artists and advisers, gave the first hint of a solution to the fragmenting values that were plaguing arts policy. Aboriginal companies and creative artists had a myriad of problems, but the authors found their way through to devise a new beginning. Citing the theatre director David Milroy, they began with the basic principle that, among Aboriginal companies, the work of 'the arts', was integral to cultural and social policy:

> Those who contribute to this policy debate might consider, as a starting point, the following questions:
>
> 1. Is the purpose of funding Indigenous performing arts to support cultural maintenance, or is it to encourage new and innovative work to emerge?

2. Who are (or should be) the audience for indigenous performing arts? Should the work be principally for Indigenous audiences, or should the work be enabled to reach mainstream audiences? If the latter is important, then how do we develop policy that will facilitate this?
3. Might the [proposed] National Indigenous Theatre Company swallow up scarce resources and marginalise the work of state-based Indigenous organisations? Or could a national flagship organisation dedicated to producing mainstage Indigenous work provide much-needed professional development and touring opportunities? [PP19, pp.58–60]

Although the debate continues today, the States now have a variety of independent Indigenous performance companies of a high standard and community focus.

Christopher Sainsbury found these same problems in the music world ten years later and addressed them in PP no.59, *Ngarra-Burria: New music and the search for an Australian sound* (2019). He was brought up in Canberra in comfortable circumstances, and teaches at the ANU School of Music. When we invited him to write a Paper about Indigenous music and musicians in the field of contemporary (new) music we were both unaware of the emotions the decision would uncover. Sainsbury is a Dharug man from Sydney and has never denied his identity; but when he opened the conversation with others during the writing of his paper, he found himself plunged into a clamour of high emotion over clan identity and the appropriation of Indigenous folk music by white Australians. He described his meeting with Peter Sculthorpe:

> 'Do you know any Aboriginal composers?' I asked. He didn't. I then confided my Aboriginality, confident that, given his history of referencing Aboriginal music materials and concepts, themes and narratives in his works, that we would have an enjoyable conversation. I assumed that he would understand the importance to me of my heritage and identity. But he simply replied: 'Really? You don't look it.' I was shocked. Whilst it was dismissive, I don't believe it was intended to be rude. [PP59, p.15]

Sainsbury stayed on track and drew attention in his Paper to his Ngarra-Burria, First People's Composers Program, whose concerts are making serious progress in uncovering a rich Australian orchestral sound.

While pressures on the arts have polarised opinion in the wider sector, Aboriginal artists have spoken with an increasingly unified voice, by connecting their art to their culture. This is a model that the arts as a whole would be well advised to emulate.

***

The fragmenting effect of market competition on the arts has been nowhere more apparent than in our major companies and educational institutions. One important initiative was the Actors' Company, a personal ambition of artistic director Robyn Nevin. Negotiations with the NSW Premier Bob Carr to establish a permanent ensemble of twelve actors at the Sydney Theatre Company had been going on since 1999. The aim had been to start the venture in 2005; but that time passed and Nevin put the project behind her.

When Carr announced the funding unexpectedly in 2006, she and the Company were caught unprepared for the task of integrating their intended experimental work into the busy timetable of a major theatre company. 'The complexity of it all was almost unbearable,' Nevin told James Waites for PP no.23, *Whatever Happened to the STC Actors' Company?* in 2010. Between 2006 and 2009 the ensemble achieved some remarkable performances, in particular of Patrick White's The Season at Sarsaparilla, referencing the TV show Big Brother, a production that brought national attention also to the director Benedict Andrews. But despite these successes the Actors' Company never recovered from Carr's impulsive act.

Artists sweat out their lives to make their ventures look easy. When those who fund them are seduced into believing that their achievements happen 'by magic', opportunities are lost in the black hole of doomed hope.

A more knowing kind of maladministration was documented by Chris Puplick in PP no.33, *Changing Times at NIDA* (2012). The School's architects, John Clark and Elizabeth Butcher, were iconic figures in the industry. They had been its guide since 1969 and had built a great school, engineered the development and management of an enormous complex of buildings on the University of NSW campus, and had delivered fine performers, designers and technicians for over forty years.

Clark retired in 2004. When Butcher followed in 2008, Puplick wrote, the past four years were 'littered with the remnants of shattered members of staff, collegiality sacrificed on the altar of corporatism.' The collapse of the family atmosphere that had been at the heart of the institution's culture was on full display in the Chairman's Report:

> Her departure was recorded in that year's Annual Report by a mere

> fourteen words in the Chairman's Report and addition of her name to the names of five other departing staff in the Director's Report. No photo of Butcher was included and no attempt was made to recognise her forty years of incomparable service. [PP33, p.22]

In 2004, Clark had been succeeded by Aubrey Mellor. When he retired, competition for the position of head of Australia's national theatre and TV school was high. The Australian list of applicants was formidable and the outcome unaccountable. Lynne Williams, an arts administrator from the UK, had little experience as a creative practitioner in the professional theatre; and only a modicum as a teacher. Her tenure only deepened the crisis in management. When she resigned, no replacement was waiting in the wings. In October 2016 the theatre director Kate Cherry accepted the post, but she too left after only two years. NIDA's decline under changing hands is a familiar story and a credit to no-one, just another loss to Australia of a valued creative asset.

In 2014 music Professor Peter Tregear put his case for bringing tertiary music qualifications into the modern world in PP no.38, *Enlightenment or Entitlement? Rethinking tertiary music education*. In 2012 he had taken on the task of moving the Canberra School of Music onto the Australian National University campus and with it a change of name and curriculum. Tertiary music, he wrote, was commonly thought of as preparing students for performance, but this conception had failed to address the shift in the ways most of us encounter music today. The failure to recognise the ubiquity of recorded music had led to a crisis in the sector that needed to be addressed, not by reducing performance tuition but by opening the students' minds to the new opportunities for performance and employment on offer today.

The Canberra School, now the ANU School of Music, was a revered institution and the prospect of change caused public outcry. In 2020 he wrote an account of the period, at the centre of which was a 'School of Music Implementation Plan' which had been delivered to him by the Vice Chancellor on his arrival and detailed a process by which the number of full-time-equivalent academic staff was to be reduced from 23.9 to 13 and professional staff from 9.23 to 7.5.

> This may explain, at least in part, why the ANU's management of the School of Music, alongside a number of other prominent discipline-centred controversies in recent years, have caused it so much grief. Changes it imposed on the School appeared to many to have been motivated by managerial priorities that seemed at best indifferent not only to the particular traditions and needs of music scholarship, but also to this discipline's capacity to contribute to the public mission of a university more generally.

A year after he left, exhausted, in 2015, a review found 'a climate of distrust, emotional stress, poor management and falling standards' within the school. Tregear returned to a teaching fellowship at Royal Holloway, University of London. He is now Dean of St Mark's College, Adelaide, and works between Australia and Europe as a singer, conductor and writer. He was replaced in 2017 by Professor Ken Lampl, a Julliard School graduate, who planned to set up a course in musical composition for film, television and video gaming. He too resigned, in 2019. The School has now embarked on a new life of contemporary musicianship under the care of the eclectic musician and composer Kim Cunio. Despite the Covid-19 pandemic, enrolments have risen.

We saw in Chris Puplick's account of NIDA's overhaul how painful the change to, or interference with, an embedded culture can be; and how it may defy the best arguments. Creators, particularly, are damaged by change or exclusion because their whole personality is engaged with the act of creation. That is why, to so many, the disappearance of Canberra's revered School of Music had been so contentious.

***

In 2013, Leigh Tabrett, former Deputy-Director General of the Department of Premier and Cabinet and Head of Arts Queensland from 2003–12, offered an insider's view of the decision-making processes of well-intentioned parliamentarians and their departmental heads, who 'didn't know what they didn't know'.

During her time as a public servant, Tabrett had led a complete reorganisation of Arts Queensland and supervised the refurbishment of the Queensland Performing Arts Centre. Following retirement, she gave us in PP no.34, *It's Culture, Stupid! Reflections of an arts bureaucrat* (2013), an entertaining account of those years. More importantly, she revealed the many pitfalls of the subsidy system that awaited parliamentarians and other innocents with too-little knowledge of arts practice, and artists who lacked the business head to recognise the dilemma.

> A question which Arts Ministers sometimes ask is: 'Why do we keep giving money to the same people year after year? When are

> they going to be able to stand on their own two feet so we can give someone else a turn?' [PP34, p.23]

Tabrett concluded her Paper more soberly by setting out seven actions that could help both sides reach a better understanding. There followed a proposal for a nationally agreed statement on the importance of culture and the purpose of public investment in it—something deserving wider attention.

In the 1970s Brisbane's long-established pro-am culture boycotted the State Government's attempts to impose a state theatre. Today Queensland has buried the memories of this notorious decade and South Brisbane has a famous cultural precinct and theatre complex of which the city is justly proud. But the old wicked problems of measuring cultural value, or of any publicly-funded project surviving the term of a single government, are still hurdles to be overcome.

That same year David Pledger produced one of our most passionately argued papers, PP no.36, *Re-valuing the Artist in the New World Order* (2013). Pledger is a leading creator, producer, writer and thinker on the value of artists to society. At a time when our last attempt to achieve a cultural policy had been shelved by yet another election, he gave sober advice on the danger of losing the arts. Artists, he wrote, were integral to making sense of our changing global landscape. They were society's antennae, the canaries in the coalmine of global change.

> In short, if you want to know where you will be in twenty years, follow an artist. If you want to get there before everyone else, fund them. [PP36, p.26]

Nations and societies that understand this today, writes Pledger, would be more culturally, socially, environmentally and economically viable.

***

In PP no.39: *The Retreat of our National Drama* (2014), Julian Meyrick called for a better research culture to revive, with deeper understanding, the past history of Australian playwriting. The work-shopping of texts has become regular practice, but, at that time, the immediate outcomes were proving disappointing. In the major companies, the time for experiment had been reduced and was being regulated by the demands of the subscription season. But in the so called 'small to medium' sector, companies, writers and directors were finding their own way.

As with the ANU School of Music, the artists coming to prominence were starting to challenge an outdated performance industry and imposing change with action. The sudden prevalence of deconstructed European classics on stage in Sydney was a symptom of a new and very personal exploration of text and performance by our senior directors and actors. These free interpretations of the classics created a furore in the media. 'What on earth is going on?' asked Meyrick.

In retrospect, what was going on was a period of maturation, for which the infrastructure of the arts was unprepared. In this thoughtful study Meyrick detailed the intentions that had brought it about and made the practical suggestion that we establish a collaborative national theatre workshop to grapple with this challenge of self-assertion.

Productive collaboration, however, was not in the air. Without warning, the Arts Minister, George Brandis, attempted to do away with the troublesome 'small to medium' sector altogether by diverting support to a fund under the Minister's direct control. Ben Eltham's PP no.48, *When the Goal Posts Move* (2016), was a towering piece of research into the extraordinary circumstances of the 'excellence raid' on Budget night, Friday 13 May 2015, which left the entire arts sector unprepared and helpless.

'The result was a bloodbath', he wrote: '65 organisations were defunded and more than a hundred that applied were also unsuccessful. The arts sector dubbed it Black Friday.'

> Some of the most famous arts companies in the country missed out [...] The defunding of a slew of Australia's best-known smaller arts companies was due to a decision made by the Abbott Government Arts Minister George Brandis, who had taken $105million in funding from the Australia Council a year before. Funding cuts bit deep. The decision came in addition to $87million slashed from the Arts portfolio in 2014. Further cuts of $52.5million were handed down in December 2015. All told, according to the Australian Labor Party's Mark Dreyfus, approximately $300million had been cut from federal cultural funding by the Coalition. [PP48, pp.1–2]

The impact of the federal cutback affected all aspects of the subsidised arts, not least the Australia Council itself. It was widely thought that it would not survive and conversation began to turn to what would happen next. The cuts had done immense damage to the Council's reputation in the industry as an independent 'arm's length' agency of government. The longer-term effects are still playing out today.

The other three Papers for 2015 were similarly directed at how to put things right by clarifying the purpose of funding the arts. My own, No. 43, *The Arts and the Common Good*, showed how decisions made at the start of subsidy had bred distrust between the arts sector and government; and how social policy had been buried under the endless tussles between the two. PP no.44, by Justin Macdonnell, *Cultural Precincts: Art or commodity?* examines the role of the long outdated distinction between 'high' and 'commercial' art in the Government's thinking; and in PP no.45: *Paying the Piper: There has to be another way*, Cathy Hunt exposes the fragility of a nation's arts funding brought down by an overnight change of Prime Minister and Cabinet; and puts forward a case for a new financial framework that draws on both government and private investment.

Justin O'Connor's PP no.47, *After the Creative Industries: Why we need a cultural economy* (2016), examines how the value of the arts has been tested through history. In the 1980s prosperity and creativity in Australia had combined in an intoxicating mix that ended with the stock market crash of 1987, after which the arts turned to the market to be its judge and saviour. O'Connor follows the rise and fall of the creative industries experiment and asserts the need for a reinvigorated cultural economy. 'What is at stake in culture', he concludes,

> as has always been, though we frequently forget it, are the great questions of ultimate value: of how we can live together and what the quality of our collective experience should be. These have not disappeared in an age of cultural abundance. They are even more urgent, as the possibility of a truly human creative society is in one way more realisable, in another as far away as it has ever been. [PP47, pp.57–8]

These last years had been drawing the arts closer and closer to the demands of the business world. In No.41, *Education and the Arts: Creativity in the promised new order* (2014), Meg Upton and Naomi Edwards dissected a new threat to the arts in the form of the Australian Curriculum, aimed at nationalising secondary education, previously the responsibility of the states. This new nationally endorsed secondary-school curriculum emphasised science, technology, engineering and mathematics (STEM) as essential subjects, while the arts and humanities were elective. This reform, to put the best face on it, was probably not intended to class the humanities as dispensable but to meet the Government's priority to raise employment—the key to which, it was assumed, lay in 'practical' subjects, not the abstract contemplations of the arts and humanities. When times are tough there's no room for imagination.

The Global Stage

Another effect of the internet was globalisation. Australian artists have a long history of leaving the country to pursue their careers. The internet did not change this trend, but it has produced a more cosmopolitan outlook. Back in 2005, in PP no.5, *Shooting Through: Australian Film and the Brain Drain*, filmmaker Storry Walton had discussed the relationship between Australian artists and the global stage:

> We have always felt ambivalent about the idea of ships and planes bearing away our talent. It has betokened a fear of the loss of native imagination, or worse, natural intelligence. It has signified regret and guilt—regret at losing our brightest and guilt at not being able

> to keep them. It has meant pride in their achievement and disdain, should they return without accolades—'They weren't really good enough, you know.' [PP5, p.4]

This fear of 'not being good enough' is familiar to older Australians and in 2005, despite government's encouragement since the 1960s, it was still hard for filmmakers to make a living here. Walton's proposed solution was to fund a program of 'sabbaticals' to encourage expatriate artists to return home to work.

However, the world was rapidly becoming a much smaller place and the parochial idea of the 'expat' has fallen out of use. Today many of our film and stage artists, concert musicians, visual artists and academics, have built their reputations overseas. They see themselves as part of a world community; and they return to Australia between jobs, because this is where they are at home.

Theatre director Neil Armfield got his start as co-director of the Nimrod Theatre in 1979, and in 1994 became the founding artistic director of its successor, the Belvoir Street Theatre Company, in its present premises. Now in his 60s, he spends most time directing opera in the UK and Europe but keeps his base in Sydney. Benedict Andrews, twenty years younger, first came to national attention at the Sydney Theatre Company in 2009 for his massive two-part adaptation of Shakespeare's history plays, under the title *The War of the Roses.* He also applied his talent to authors like Tennessee Williams, including a famous *A Streetcar Named Desire.* He now lives in Reykjavic and works throughout Europe and the US, directing opera, film and classic drama.

Barrie Kosky, born and raised in Melbourne of European Jewish parentage, has shared an ambivalent relationship with his native land. His Australian career has been a continuing source of controversy. In his twenties he made his mark as artistic director of a spectacular 1996 Adelaide Festival, after which he made his home in Europe, firstly at the Vienna Schauspielhaus. He is now among the first rank of directors in the northern hemisphere. His international reputation rests mainly on opera and includes work at the Bayreuth, Frankfurt, Glyndebourne and Los Angeles opera houses. The catalogue of his work in Europe is prodigious—all but a fraction are opera classics.

The director Simon Stone, still in his 30s, lives where the work is. He was born of Australian parents in Basel, Switzerland, and grew up in Melbourne and Cambridge. In 2007 he founded the Hayloft Project in Melbourne, and later transferred to the Belvoir Street Theatre. His adaptation of Ibsen's *The Wild Duck*, staged inside a Perspex box, was the cause of both admiration and scandal in Sydney for its startling Australian reinterpretation of Ibsen's characters. In 2015 he returned to Europe and now works mainly in Amsterdam.

It will not have escaped the reader's notice that these directors are all male. Our female directors have had a tougher journey; but two who stand out on their own terms are Gale Edwards and Lindy Hume.

Edwards began her career in Adelaide with the youth theatre Energy Connection; and directed for the state theatre companies until she moved to London in the 1990s. In 1996 she directed the London revival of *Jesus Christ Superstar*, which transferred to Broadway in 2000, and won an Emmy award for the television production. Since then she has directed for the Royal Shakespeare Company and the Shakespeare Theatre Company in Washington, DC; and in 2003 she directed the premiere in

Sydney of the musical *The Boy from* Oz and Sondheim's *Sweeney Todd,* for which she received Helpmann awards.

Lindy Hume has for years travelled the globe directing opera. From 1992 to 1996 she was director of the Western Australian Opera; then of the Victorian Opera from 2004 to 2007 and thereafter the Perth and Sydney festivals to 2012. In 2004 she chose to settle on the south coast of New South Wales and join the community of artists gathering there. In PP no.50, *Restless Giant: Changing cultural values in regional Australia*, she described her way of life and how she had made the leap from one reality to another:

> In the decade since [coming here], regional Australia has been a constant inspiration and focus. Coming home to the beautiful South Coast and my local community has sustained me, grounded me, providing aesthetic inspiration, a sanctuary for reflection. Community values have informed my work and identity as Festival Director of Sydney Festival and Artistic Director of Opera Queensland, and as a freelance director in Australia, Europe, New Zealand and America. [PP50, p.4]

Government has also encouraged Australians to expand their careers by going abroad. In 2012 veteran Asia-watchers Alison Carroll and Carrillo Gantner examined the strategy of 'soft diplomacy' employed by the Department of Foreign Affairs and Trade in PP no.31, *Finding a Place on the Asian Stage*. Funding stars like Cate Blanchett to tour an Australian production of a world classic, they argued, might be good for government kudos but did little for trade relations. They proposed instead the creation of an Australian International Cultural Agency to oversee policy, programs and funding. Its responsibilities would include not only art and performance but international education, public festivals and events, collaborations, the establishment of cultural centres in major cities and programs directed towards the international exchange of talent and knowledge.

This paper did not bring the kind of thoughtful response it deserved. Cultural policy was not top of mind in Canberra at that moment. Politics had become personal and vindictive following the dramatic 'coup' that saw Kevin Rudd replaced by Julia Gillard. Gillard, in turn, fell victim to factional in-fighting in a series of leadership spills. The extraordinary abuse on social media to which she was subjected shone a spotlight on the 'trolling' endured by women in the public domain, but was eclipsed by her 'misogyny speech', addressed to Opposition Leader Tony Abbott, in 2012. In 2013 she lost office and retired, unbroken and visibly unscathed; and has continued to contribute skilfully to public policy and life. But it was an ugly, exhausting period, full of auguries. Since the election in 2016 of Donald Trump as President of the United States, Australia's foreign affairs in Asia have been dominated by America's rivalry with China.

***

Artists were also drawn abroad by commercial success. The entrepreneurial spirit, fostered by the economic changes, policy reforms and technological advances since 2000, found its outlet in a wave of musical and dance theatre. Australians are good at music and dance shows: at performing them and attending them. The Bangarra Dance Theatre has won a national award almost annually since its founding in 1991; and shows like *Bran Nue Dae* (1990), *Tap Dogs* (1995) and *The Boy from Oz* (1998), were home grown works that ran, and continued to run, in Australia and overseas for years. This was only the beginning.

A key figure in this efflorescence was the dynamic producer Baz Luhrmann, who gained national attention straight out of NIDA. Luhrmann's *Strictly Ballroom* began life as a student production at NIDA in 1984, played around Australia and then became a film. By 1992, his partnership with designer Catherine Martin was merging art, fashion and culture, to create the trademark style of their 'Red Curtain Trilogy': *Strictly Ballroom, William Shakespeare's Romeo + Juliet* (1996) and *Moulin Rouge* (2001). These films carried the theatrical sensibility of the stage onto the screen and around the world.

In 2009, Stephan Elliott and Alan Scott took the opposite direction, transforming the film of *Priscilla Queen of the Desert* into a stage show. It opened in Sydney in 2006, played London's West End in 2009, and continued to tour in Britain and the US until halted, like Tim Minchin's *Matilda* for the Royal Shakespeare Company, and P. J. Hogan, Kate Miller-Heidke and Keir Nuttal's *Murial's Wedding*, by the ubiquitous Covid-19 virus.

By 2016 the adventurous directors and designers of the 1990s were in their 50s, independent cosmopolitans who used the internet to make their connections. Their work spanned opera, musicals, dance, circus and drama that toured Europe and occasionally North America and Asia.

Musicals require an enormous infrastructure of space, equipment, skills and talent. In 2015, John Senczuk, an imaginative and versatile theatre-maker with a healthy respect for the business side of the arts, outlined a plan in PP no.42, *The Time is Ripe for the Great Australian Musical,* for creating our own musicals industry by pooling the resources of Australia's production companies. The timing of the publication was unlucky. It was February 2015 and three months later the Australia Council's expected funding was plundered for the next four years. Senczuk's plan attracted producers but in the uneasy climate was judged too risky. In 2020 many large shows around the world have been brought to a standstill by the pandemic, while others have converted risk into opportunity.

Hasty laws and political obstruction, risk aversion and embarrassment at commercial success, still dog Australian creative enterprise. There is such loneliness about the way we work in the arts. 2015 saw the death of many hopes for lack of that quality of generosity and collaboration of which we are so capable. Given the success of other endeavours, this outcome was disappointing.

***

Over 2016–17 we published a sub-series, *The Professionals,* which gave insight into what it had been like for individuals to live through the tumultuous changes we had been documenting for more than a decade. As with all the Papers, these were for me an illumination.

In PP no.46, *The Designer: Decorator or dramaturg?* Stephen Curtis describes how his work as a stage designer for a major theatre company requires agility to find visual expression for the words on the page and synthesis with the director and actors' own imagination. There had been a time when the designer was not on the payroll until all the production choices had been made; and was required to do no more than provide a picture frame for the production. Today his work is integrated and extensive.

At the Sydney Theatre Company Curtis was drawn into Neil Armfield's creative team and in 2016 designed what became the much-applauded, emotionally-grounded bush setting of the play *The Secret River*, adapted by Andrew Bovell from the prize-winning novel by Kate Grenville.

In PP no.49, *The Lighting Designer: What is 'good' lighting?* Nigel Levings told how he began work at His Majesty's Theatre in Melbourne as a youth hired to keep the lights on. With each job he learned new skills until, by 2016, he was winning international awards and controlling giant digital lighting desks in the great theatres around the world. The best lighting, in his view, goes unnoticed but enables the characters on stage to be effectively seen to the back of the gallery. (Another kind of theatrical 'magic'.)

PP no.52 *Putting Words in Their Mouths: The playwright and screenwriter at work* (2017), was the work of the prolific stage and screen writer, Andrew Bovell. Bovell first made his mark in the spartan conditions of the Melbourne Workers' Theatre and has had notable stage and screen success, here and abroad, with plays like *After Dinner, Speaking in Tongues* (which became the film *Lantana*) and *When the Rain Stops Falling*. His recent plays have achieved a pattern of extended life in the UK, Europe and the USA; and he now spends much of his year working abroad. His recent family drama, *Things I know to be True,* has already been successful in the UK and America. His screenplays include *Strictly Ballroom, Edge of Darkness, Lantana* and *Head On.*

All these personal accounts of professional lives spent in the arts, tell stories of artistic survival. In PP no.53, *The Jobbing Actor: Rules of engagement*, Lex Marinos described what that means for actors:

> How to define the jobbing actor? Not the handful who find fame and fortune and power. The ones that audiences pay to see. I want to write about the vast majority of actors, the ones that struggle to stay employed. [PP53, p.12]

Marinos is Australian-born of Greek parents and has earned his living almost entirely in this country. In 1970 he was cast in the pantomime *Hamlet on Ice* at the fledgling Nimrod Street Theatre (now Griffin) and quickly crossed into radio and television at the ABC. In the 1980s he spent four years playing the Italian-Australian character 'Bruno' in the TV comedy *Kingswood Country.*

> I maintained that as he was born here he should speak with a normal Australian accent. I was sick of seeing, and playing, stereotypical 'wogs'—not that there were many then in our Anglo-centric television shows. The producers/writers agreed with me, and it proved a smart move. [PP53, p.30]

Working in an unregulated industry takes a huge toll on the health of actors, both mental and physical, and Marinos has some advice on that. Acting schools have begun preparing their graduates for the challenges of life as jobbing actors. They are better trained than they have ever been, but it remains a precarious career:

> Apart from their acting skills they will have also been trained in marketing and technology, financial planning and legal requirements, lifestyle and resilience skills. They will have a show reel, a voice tape and a five-year plan.[...] All will have just a year to establish themselves

before the marketplace receives the next three hundred graduates. [PP53, p.66]

The authors of *The Professionals* share one overwhelming characteristic: devotion to their work and a willingness to go to the limit every time. Levings says that the aim of the best lighting is to go unnoticed. The same can be said of the best acting, dancing and writing: the outcome, when it is good, appears effortless. That is the paradox of being a performer.

Mark Williams, a Melbourne lawyer with a long professional interest in the welfare of the creative sector, details the eccentric conditions under which performers work, and their irregular relationship to our health and welfare services, in PP no.56, *Falling Through the Gaps: Artists' health and welfare* (2018). These support systems have been upgraded or re-regulated at intervals, he explains, but at every turn the artist/performer has eluded the benefits. In the past, an actor who won a major role in a television series, and was required to be on call, could have expected a fulltime salary for the whole of the contract period. Today the practice of paying actors only for the hours they work can reduce the period of their employment on a major production to weeks or even a few days.

How is it fair that the spectacular global success of our entrepreneurs should be at the cost of the workers who star in them? These advances have been built on the invisible talents of our local jobbing artists. To be innovative, artists need the investment of government grants, but to survive and succeed they need a living wage.

Division and Cultural Unity

The first Platform Paper to gain mainstream media coverage was Lee Lewis' PP no.13, *Cross-Racial Casting: Changing the face of Australian Theatre* in 2007. She earned her MFA in Acting from Columbia University and worked as an actor and director in Manhattan before returning to Australia at a time when finding work depended more than ever on whom you knew. She had been unemployed for over a year when she confided to me one day that she was disturbed by the whiteness of the productions she had seen on stage since her return. Why did the casting not reflect the variety of faces she saw in the street? The outcome was the Paper she wrote for us. As expected, the media made a meal of her observations and Lewis faced the possibility of never working in the theatre again.

Seven years later, I asked her to reflect on her decision to speak out. She responded generously:

> The Currency House Platform Paper I wrote was the hardest thing I have ever done and the best. Personally and professionally, the effort and the repercussions shaped my work and my career path in great and awful ways and I believe will continue to do so for the rest of my life. The commitment to the articulation of private observation in a public and permanent sphere both forced a clarity I had not faced before and courage I had not anticipated needing.
>
> The reaction to the paper was severe and enlightening. It enabled me to meet a level of Australian thought makers and theatre makers in a new way and to form conversations which continue to this day. I had to learn how to speak the sentences I had written in the face of people who alternately opposed and celebrated the ideas. I met sides of people I had not wanted to realise existed. I was discussing

institutional racism but encountered first-hand evidence of personal racism in embedded and unexpected places.

The paper keeps me in touch with my fierce younger self. Every day I am haunted by my ability to change the status quo or maintain it. The paper means I will never be able to let myself off the hook. It was written as a direct appeal to directors to acknowledge the difference they can make in shaping the visual and aural imagination of this country to long-term political effect. I am aware of every instance where I fail in my own productions to push the conversation further. As I get older I know more about why different decisions are made—why various casting decisions are made; why the cast you hoped for is not the cast you have. I go to bed at times knowing that while I have made a good production I have failed my younger voice that says every production is an opportunity to change expectations. I understand the compromise process more, but I do not live with it well. I don't credit the paper with changing anything—words don't make change, actions inspired by those words do. I still look forward to the time when this paper is redundant.

Despite the reaction of the media, by the time Lewis's Paper was published she was directing at the Sydney Opera House. In 2012 she was appointed director of the Griffin Theatre and in 2019 artistic director of Queensland Theatre. Not immediately but, gradually, on stage and in film and television, brown and Asian faces began to take their place in the repertoire. Today their appearance in 'white' roles goes unremarked. This change has enabled fine actors like Deborah Mailman, Wayne Blair and Aaron Pedersen to take on the roles their skills merit and gain the admiration they deserve. They have made a difference and been awarded for it.

***

Not all the Papers we have published have received a mention in this essay. But all of them deserve repeated reading—for their motivation, their good advice and their determination to work for a better future in the face of a bleak outlook.

Since the Australia Council was established in 1968 to bring value and recognition to our arts workers, the arts have been weakened by strategies of divide and conquer: division into genres, major and minor arts organisations, and even the entrepreneurialism encouraged by the ABN, has pitted art forms, companies and individual artists against each other in competition for the arts dollar.

Wesley Enoch's PP no.40, *Take Me to Your Leader: The dilemma of cultural leadership* (2014), speaks for his fellow artists; and is compulsory reading for anyone trying to understand what has gone so wrong in the arts sector; how these curious gaps have appeared in our cultural understanding and what the consequences might be:

> In the 1970s, with the establishment of the Australia Council, we saw the formalising of some kind of official culture. Funding provided a framework within which to experiment and explore ideas that examine Australian life and reflect our own aspirations. The question today is whether the idea of a state-sanctioned culture has led to the taming and silencing of the rambunctious dissenting mob that had ruled our performing arts for over two centuries. In the search for the approval of the public purse, have we lost our wit and charm, the art of surviving through persuasion, our critical purpose and our taste for the popular? [PP40, p.13]

Public funding has divided the arts, and their defences have been systematically dismantled. The funding bodies' emphasis on art form has divided and narrowed the interests that artists hold in common. This has meant that problems have been discussed in terms of outcomes. The Australia Council's creation in 1999 of the Major Performing Arts Group (AMPAG) divided the territory between a privileged group of 28 established arts organisations and the 'small-to-medium' sector. This was a further separation between big and small, and was similarly interpreted as a division between those companies who would be supported to survive, and the rest. It was, of course, controversial from the start and it led inexorably to what must be the lowest point in the Arts/Government relationship: the moment when Minister Brandis siphoned off the money for the small to medium sector and AMPAG stayed silent. Despite their privilege, no-one was prepared to gamble their company's livelihood, or their own. Wesley Enoch names himself among them. AMPAG has now been disbanded but the problem of indifference, between artists and the arts bureaucracy, remains manifest.

We need to find a way to unify without suppressing diversity. Artists need to see what they do as an expression of culture and society first, and as a product to be marketed second. We must turn back to our old strengths: bringing people together and allowing them to feel part of society by enjoying the pleasures of their culture.

The problems of the arts should be discussed in terms of what artists need for a productive life: sustained employment, health, advocacy, funding priorities and social recognition. Actors lost their most powerful industrial defence—the face of celebrity representing their rights—when in 1992 Actors' Equity merged with the Journalists' Association, to become the Media Alliance. Celebrity has been harnessed to promotion. Some essential work in the public sphere that Equity once did (or failed to do) has now been picked up by Theatre Network Australia.

The global crises we face at the moment are an opportunity to reposition the arts in relation to society and the economy. They have forced us to turn inwards—no international travel, no interstate travel, no crowds, the things that have fed economic growth and the rise of globalisation to date—and we have learned, 'We're all in this together'. At the highest level, research companies have joined forces to find a vaccine. Former competitors are sharing their resources. Ruthless market competition and self-reliant individualism will no longer serve.

It is easy to blame the regulators and to see the arts worker as an eccentric, vulnerable figure that public power and policy have failed. But the pattern I still see, after trudging through the stages of our history and watching how the fortunes of creative people have followed the money and its opportunities, is that from the outset the decision of the Australian Government to take responsibility for the arts sector was made under terms that were fatally flawed.

Maybe at the time the idea of an Australia Council for the Arts was just a welcome distraction for the baby-boomers who had reached their majority and were up for the Vietnam conscription ballot. Regulation was loose, arts practitioners welcomed the funding and the arts blossomed into the New Wave. In the first years of the Council its field officers were arts workers who travelled the country and became our mentors, quietly showing us how to design our project and fill in the application form. Then their travel was halted. Perhaps the cause was the oil crisis of the early

70s, but whatever the reason, within four years the bureaucrats were in charge. Vital initiatives were overruled by people with more clout, and gradually the needs of the patron and that of the artist, diverged. We who were observers and in a position to call for a rewind on the original criteria missed our chance

Nevertheless, the Australia Council has transformed civil society. Today we have arts institutions, performance and teaching facilities, theatres and concert halls to admire. Would they be here, had it been left to the private sector? Or would it have been done differently? By now, the creative sector should long ago have been written into social policy. It should have an Arts Minister and a Department staffed by arts workers, dedicated to forward planning and fostering collaborative enterprises: a Department like that proposed by Alison Carroll and Carrillo Gantner in PP no.31, *Finding a Place on the Asian Stage* (2012).

Instead of persisting in the endless, competitive pursuit of excellence, why not evaluate the needs of a healthy arts sector and set about putting them in place? Why not consider every one of the many innovative plans proposed by our authors over the past sixteen years that 'fall outside the guidelines'? A first step would be to change the language: define individual Australia Council grants, now seen as money with which to produce art, as money for cultural research.

Since 2000, artists have been too frightened to speak out in case they lose an elusive chance for work. Don't be afraid to say you are out of work. Today more than half the country is out of work; and rethinking their priorities. What have we got to lose?

Reforming the arts requires good advisers, good records, a collaborative strategy, funds to experiment and a living wage. My hope is that, as we come out of this dark period in our history, Australia might take the lead in the challenge to make the world a kinder, more inclusive place than it has been. By living too fast we have come too quickly to the end of the road. 'A Change for the Better' is the Platform Papers' motto. All we need is the courage to make it.

Endnotes

1 Harry Lime is a fictional American survivalist played by Orson Welles in the British film noir *The Third Man* (1949), written by Graham Greene, directed by Carol Reed, and set in a grim post-war Vienna. The Ferris-wheel conversation between Lime and his childhood friend Holly Martins (Joseph Cotton) is legendary in film history. In 1999 *The Third Man* was voted the greatest British film of all time by the British Film Institute.

2 Election speech. Delivered in Sydney by John Howard, 28 October 2001. Museum of Australian Democracy, 'Election Speeches'. https://electionspeeches.moadoph.gov.au

3 Its name was changed to Australian Broadcasting Corporation under the Act of 1983, marking an important transition away from the culture of the BBC.

4 Amanda Meade. 'ABC loses more than $783m funding since 2016 when Coalition made its first cuts–report' *Guardian*. 4 May, 2020. https://www.theguardian.com/media/2020/may/04/abc-loses-793m-funding-since-2014-when-coalition-made-its-first-cuts-report

5 'The Damnation of Ruddock' in Platform Papers no. 10, *Satire—or Sedition? The threat to national insecurity*, 2005, pp.44–50.

6 Chris Puplick. *Changing Times at NIDA*, Platform Paper no. 33, 2012, p.4.

7 Ibid, p.21.

8 Ibid, p.16.

9 Peter Tregear. 'Time to face the Music?' *Demos Journal*, 31 January 2020. http://demosjournal.com.

10 Emma Macdonald, 'Australian National University's School of Music "poorly managed by the university at all levels"'. *Canberra Times.* 2 May 2016. Review by Public Commissioner Andrew Podger of the ANU School. https://www.canberratimes.com.au/story/6050121/australian-national-universitys-school-of-music-poorly-managed-by-the-university-at-all-levels/

11 Julia Gillard's speech at Question Time on 9 October 2012 began: 'I rise to oppose the motion moved by the Leader of the Opposition [Tony Abbott]. And in so doing I say to the Leader of the Opposition I will not be lectured about sexism and misogyny by this man. I will not. And the Government will not be lectured about sexism and misogyny by this man. Not now, not ever.' The speech was later declared the most watched speech on TV that year.

12 In the possession of the author.

13 Wesley Enoch. *Take Me to Your Leader: The dilemma of cultural leadership.* Platform Paper no. 40, 2014, p.29.

About the Author

KATHARINE BRISBANE is a writer and publisher who co-founded Currency Press, Australia's performing arts publisher, with her late husband, Dr Philip Parsons, in 1971. She was a theatre critic for 21 years, including a period as national critic of the *Australian* (1967–1974), a time of radical change that saw the rise of contemporary drama, film and music in Australia. She has published widely on the history and nature of Australian theatre. She remained publisher of Currency Press until her retirement in 2001 and at that time established Currency House, Inc., a not-for-profit association with the brief to assert the value of the performing arts in public life and raise the level of debate.

She was a founder in 1972 of the Australian National Playwrights' Conference and was Chair from 1985–1990. In 1991 to celebrate Currency Press's first twenty years she edited *Entertaining Australia*, a social history of the performing arts. In 1993 Katharine and Philip were both awarded the AM for their work as publishers of Australian drama. Dr Parsons died the same month and Katharine completed the production of his encyclopaedia, *Companion to Theatre in Australia*, published in 1995. She holds honorary doctorates from the University of NSW and the University of WA, and many awards for her writing and publishing, including the Dorothy Crawford Award by the Australian Writers' Guild for outstanding service to the Australian playwright, and lifetime achievement awards from Melbourne's Green

Room, the Sydney Critics Circle, and in 2009 a Special Award from the NSW Premier in the Literary Awards list for services to Australian literature and theatre.

From 1994 she was editor for the South Pacific for the *World Encyclopaedia of Contemporary Theatre* (Routledge), for which she also wrote the Australian entry. *Volume 5: Asia and the Pacific* was published in 1998. She has written widely in books and journals and a collection of her writings, *Not Wrong, Just Different: Observations on the rise of the contemporary theatre*, was published in 2005.

Katharine Brisbane has two children: Nicholas, a film-maker, and Harriet, an artist and independent researcher; and two granddaughters.

Platform Papers, 2004–21

First published July 2004

PP1 *'Our ABC'—A Dying Culture?* Martin Harrison

PP2 *Survival of the Fittest: The artist versus the corporate world,* Christopher Latham

2005

PP3 *Trapped by the Past: Why our theatre is facing paralysis,* Julian Meyrick

PP4 *The Myth of the Mainstream: Politics and the performing arts in Australia today,* Robyn Archer

PP5 *Shooting Through: Australian film and the brain drain,* Storry Walton

PP6 *Art in a Cold Climate: Rethinking the Australia Council,* Keith Gallasch

2006

PP7 *Does Australia Need a Cultural Policy?* David Throsby

PP8 *Body for Hire? The state of dance in Australia,* Amanda Card

PP9 *What Price a Creative Economy?* Stuart Cunningham

PP10 *Satire—or Sedition? The threat to national insecurity,* Jonathan Biggins

2007

PP11 *A Regional State of Mind: Making art outside metropolitan Australia*, Lyndon Terracini

PP12 *Film in the Age of Digital Distribution: The challenge for Australian content*, Richard Harris

PP13 *Cross-racial Casting: Changing the face of Australian theatre*, Lee Lewis

PP14 *Who Profits from the Arts? Taking the measure of culture*, Kay Ferres and David Adair

2008

P15 *A Sustainable Arts Sector: What will it take?* Cathy Hunt and Phyllida Shaw

PP16 *The Permanent Underground: Australian contemporary jazz in the new Millennium*, Peter Rechniewski

PP17 *What is an Australian Play? Have we failed our ethnic writers?* Chris Mead

PP18 *Getting Heard: Achieving an effective arts advocacy*, Chris Puplick

2009

PP19 *'Your Genre is Black': Indigenous performing arts and policy* Hilary Glow and Katya Johanson

PP20 *Beethoven or Britney: The great divide in music education*, Robert Walker

PP21 *Television: What will rate in the new tomorrow?* Ian David

PP22 *Copyright, Collaboration and the future of dramatic authorship*, Brent Salter

2010 (one paper cancelled)

PP23 *Whatever Happened to the STC Actors Company?* James Waites

PP24 *The Digital Playing Fields: New rulz for film art and performance*, Shilo McClean

PP25 *Moving Across Disciplines: Dance in the twenty-first century*, Erin Brannigan

2011

PP26 *Not Just an Audience: Young people transforming our theatre*, Lenine Bourke and Mary Ann Hunter

PP27 *Hello, World! Promoting the arts on the web*, Robert Reid

PP28 *The Fall and Rise of the VCA*, Richard Murphet

PP29 *Democracy versus Creativity in Australian Classical Music*, Nicole Canham

2012

P30 *Indig-curious: Who can play Aboriginal roles?* Jane Harrison

PP31 *Finding a place on the Asian stage*, Alison Carroll and Carrillo Gantner

PP32 *History is Made at Night: Live music in Australia*, Clinton Walker

PP33 *Changing Times at NIDA*, Chris Puplick

2013

PP34 *It's Culture, Stupid! Reflections of an arts bureaucrat*, Leigh Tabrett

PP35 *The Music of Place: Reclaiming the practice*, Jon Rose

PP 36 *Re-valuing the Artist in the New World Order*, David Pledger

PP37 *Not at a Cinema Near You: Australia's film distribution problem*, Lauren Carroll Harris

2014

PP38 *Enlightenment or Entitlement? Rethinking tertiary music education*, Peter Tregear

PP39 *The Retreat of our National Drama*, Julian Meyrick

PP40 *Take Me to Your Leader: The dilemma of cultural leadership*, Wesley Enoch

PP41 *Education and the arts: Creativity in the promised new order*, Meg Upton with Naomi Edwards

2015

PP42 *The Time Is Ripe for the Great Australian Musical*, John Senczuk

PP43 *The Arts and the Common Good*, Katharine Brisbane
PP44 *Cultural Precincts: Art or commodity?* Justin Macdonnell
PP45 *Paying the Piper: There has to be another way*, Cathy Hunt

2016

PP46 *The Designer: Decorator or dramaturg?* Stephen Curtis
PP47 *Why We Need a Cultural Economy*, Justin O'Connor
PP48 *When the Goal Posts Move*, Ben Eltham
PP49 *The Lighting Designer: What is 'good' lighting*, Nigel Levings

2017

PP50 *Restless Giant: Changing cultural values in regional Australia*, Lindy Hume
PP51 *Missing in Action: The ABC and Australia's screen culture*, Kim Dalton
PP52 *Putting Words in their Mouths: The playwright and screenwriter at work*, Andrew Bovell
PP53 *The Jobbing Actor: Rules of engagement*, Lex Marinos

2018

PP54 *Young People and the Arts: An agenda for change*, Sue Giles
PP55 *Art, Politics, Money: Revisiting Australia's cultural policy*, David Throsby
PP56 *Falling Through the Gaps: Our artists' health and welfare*, Mark RW Williams
PP57 *Cultural Justice and the right to thrive*, Scott Rankin

2019

PP58 *The Changing Landscape of Australian Documentary*, Tom Zubrycki
PP59 *Ngarra-Burria: New music and the search for an Australian sound*, Christopher Sainsbury
PP60 *Capturing the Vanishing; A choreographer and film*, Sue Healey
PP61 *Criticism, Performance and the need for conversation*, Alison Croggon

2020

PP62 *Performing Arts Markets and their Conundrums*, Justin Macdonnell

2021

PP63 *On the Lessons of History*, Katharine Brisbane

CURRENCY HOUSE INC.

Currency House is a not-for-profit organisation devoted to promoting wider understanding of the work of artists and creative practitioners and how it contributes to Australia's social and political life.

Correspondence should be addressed to:
The Editor
The New Platform Papers
P. O. Box 2270
Strawberry Hills NSW 2012 Australia
Email: info@currencyhouse.org.au

Typeset in Garamond.
Layout design by Emma Bennetts.
Production by Currency Press Pty Ltd.
Printed in Australia by Ligare Book Printers, Riverwood.

The paper used to produce this book comes from wood grown in sustainable forests.